The Stories We Tell

The Stories We Tell

Math, Race, Bias, and Opportunity

Valerie N. Faulkner, Patricia L. Marshall, and Lee V. Stiff

ROWMAN & LITTLEFIELD
Lanham • Boulder • New York • London

Published by Rowman & Littlefield
An imprint of The Rowman & Littlefield Publishing Group, Inc.
4501 Forbes Boulevard, Suite 200, Lanham, Maryland 20706
www.rowman.com

6 Tinworth Street, London SE11 5AL

British Library Cataloguing in Publication Information Available

Library of Congress Cataloging-in-Publication Data Available

ISBN 9781475841626 (cloth : alk. paper)
ISBN 9781475841640 (electronic)

♾ ™ The paper used in this publication meets the minimum requirements of American
National Standard for Information Sciences Permanence of Paper for Printed Library
Materials, ANSI/NISO Z39.48-1992.

Contents

Acknowledgments

We have many people to thank for their support and encouragement of our work. Most notably, we would like to thank Tom F. Koerner, vice president/publisher of education titles at Rowman & Littlefield, who read an article we published in *Phi Delta Kappan*, recognized a fuller story was waiting to be told, and invited us to expand our ideas into a book. Our thanks extend also to others at Rowman & Littlefield for their efforts throughout this process.

We would like also to thank Robert Q. Berry, Danny Martin, Marielle Myers, William "Bill" Tate, and Dorothy Y. White for their inspiring work on issues of education and social justice and for taking the time to read advance copies of this book.

Heartfelt thanks and deep gratitude are extended from us to a host of colleagues and graduate students whose individual contributions are too numerous to detail here but whose names we would be remiss not to list. They are Lisa Bass, Cathy Crossland, Anna Egalite, Emily Elrod, Regina Gavin Williams, Joanna Greer Koch, Erin Huggins, John Lee, John Nietfeld, Jessica Wagstaff, Temple Walkowiak, and Kelly Womack.

Valerie N. Faulkner
Patricia L. Marshall
Lee V. Stiff

PERSONAL THANKS

I am so thankful for having the opportunity to work with Patricia and Lee on this book. Lee inspired my approach to the work back in 2005 and has been a provocative, fun, and inspiring mentor and colleague ever since. Patricia influenced my life beginning in 1993 when I was fortunate to have her for a graduate class. Our daylong sessions these past couple of years have been a great source of joy for me as she has modeled, once again, the power of precision, ideas, language, and message.

Thanks to my most dedicated allies in spirit and "readers" of this book, Jeff Faulkner, Suzanne Faulkner, Elizabeth MacWilliams, Michele Miller, Kathleen Owens, Kim Talikoff, Sue Parent, Jacki Russell, and Nancy Spencer. Finally, I thank Jenn Smith, the most voracious and discriminating reader I know. As it is her opinion that matters most to me in all things, I am not only thankful for her support but also for her continued faith in me, in this work, and in our life together.

—VNF

Special thanks to Professor K. S. Havner for his support during this project. Also, thanks to the *Women in Science and Engineering* (WISE) group at Universidad San Francisco de Quito (including the *wise guys* and the *otherwise*), who all expressed interest in learning more about how high-quality early learning opportunities in mathematics really are critical to who gets to be part of "the wise."

—PLM

I want to thank my longtime friend and colleague, Janet Johnson, of Edstar Analytics. She has always been the foundation of my capacity to grapple with complex and detailed data sets about the plight of underserved student populations. We have worked closely for more than 25 years to frame issues and provide solutions related to better serving the needs of all children and providing every student with high-quality mathematics and mathematics instruction.

—LVS

Introduction

For decades now we have heard the story of a racial achievement gap related to health, economic status, and school performance. History tells us that gaps in student academic achievement can largely be tied to public policy and the disparate, and inequitable, living conditions these policies create. [1]

At the same time, we know that student experiences in schools also affect student achievement. As educators we seek to understand our impact on students once they arrive at school. While we acknowledge the broader issues that affect student outcomes, in these pages we explore the "achievement gap" story as it relates to *issues we can control within the walls of the school*. In particular, we explore school-based professional decision-making and patterns of practice that affect student mathematical opportunities—and thereby serve to maintain "the gap."

The mathematics achievement gap, the story goes, describes something about students, something about color or socioeconomic status, something about low academic performance. The math gap story has a visual, statistics, a past, and a present.

The math gap story (and the racial gap story in particular) is by now, most certainly, "a thing." It is an accepted part of beliefs about students and schools. The gap is, shall we say, built into the operating system, and it orients many of us to the fundamental nature of the structure and reality of student performance.

In this gap story, the gap is that space between the academically blessed and the academically bleak. A visual of two different-colored lines (one high and one low) running across a Cartesian plane validates the idea of the gap. In keeping with the gap visual, educators set about trying to eliminate the gap by providing support services to that lower line of children.

1

But what if the conception is wrong? *What if the students are not the problem to be fixed?*

With this book as a lens, we aim to guide you through this gapped landscape and tell a different story about students, educators, opportunity, and math performance. We go in different directions to find a forward path. We look wide with telescopes to examine how, for instance, seemingly innocuous decisions made at the start of a child's schooling affect that same child's successes in later grades, and in life. With opera glasses we see what's on stage at the school and child level. How is the story affecting students now? What happens to student mathematical opportunity when schools step outside the gap story and instead broker solutions?

Extending this metaphor, we also home in on a microscopic level to consider how the details of professional decision-making affect student opportunity. To be sure, educators are not alone in making critical decisions that affect people's lives. Indeed, both intended and unintended consequences occur from decision-making in many contexts. Therefore, to illustrate the widespread nature of this phenomenon, we explore decision-making across a diverse collection of social and professional realms. Our goal is to create a backdrop for understanding how unrelated assumptions can, and often do, affect the quality of the decisions individuals make. In short, while we focus our story on educators, the themes and ideas we highlight are common to many professions and vocational fields.

This book is also about data and reactions to it. How are educators using data for the professional decision-making found in education? We seek to free the data and use it effectively, by disentangling it from the stories educators have told themselves about a gap. We also aim to free the data so it can fill in details and tell a new story about communities, educators, ideas, and, most importantly, students.

We illustrate how understanding data can mitigate bias and why this is sometimes so hard to do. As in other professions, educators must negotiate conceptions and biases that affect their thinking. We believe educators can and should strive to implement better protocols that allow them to acquire awareness of such biases and find appropriate data to inform their decisions. By better understanding the data they choose, educators can write a different story, one that better reflects the realities of their students. Hand in hand, the new story and the data can guide the professional judgment of educators to effectively and equitably affect the children and communities they serve.

As noted above, a key part of this new story relates to debunking the visual of an academic gap. We believe that, once the use of an *average* to symbolize, justify, or make decisions about individuals is understood as a *farce*, then everything changes. Once we free the data from this misunderstanding, the landscape created, the capacities of students, and the quest for equitable solutions look different.

The stories we tell are grounded in the complex and diverse world of public schools. Educators in our public schools work every day to teach the nation's children, and they do so in conditions that render their job, at times, a selfless act of persistence and kindness. Public school educators are not the antagonists in this story; they are the people who strive to make a difference.[2] This book tells a story that is not about a failure of educators but a failure of culture.

Throughout the book we recast the so-called achievement gap as a story of decisions and opportunity. These pages are intended as a guide for thinking deeply about assumptions, beliefs, and actions as they relate to opportunity in mathematics. What's more, we make clear how the "small" decisions of classroom teachers have large cumulative effects on societal understandings and how large, district-wide actions affect individual student outcomes.

Finally, this book is about how decisions affect students differently and, unfortunately, in predictable ways that often are coupled with race and economic class differentials in the larger society. In the United States, with its undeniable history (and the continued reality) of stratified opportunities, these topics can be difficult to explore. Our stories and examples may elicit recognition of the realities of injustice for some, whereas, among others, these same stories may elicit difficult feelings of defensiveness or regret. Given this, we hope you find that our presentation is one that provides you, the reader, a safe place to explore these ideas freely and openly as one would any complicated but compelling story.

NOTES

1. See Rothstein, R. (2017). *The color of law: A forgotten history of how our government segregated America.* New York, NY: Liveright.

2. Indeed, the book *The public school advantage: Why public schools outperform private schools* (Lubienski & Lubienski, 2013) details how our nation's public school children outperform students in private schools in mathematics at virtually all points of comparison.

I

The Gap-Maker

Chapter One

The Farce of Early Identification

The First Story of Gap-Making

Human ability at exceptional levels is a delight to behold.[1] Whether it manifests as a brilliant chess strategy, a stunning feat of athleticism, or a flawless piano recital, people value exceptionality. Often, it is treated as a scarce commodity to be praised, celebrated, and even rewarded. When the hint of exceptionality is present among the very young, it is especially lauded. Many adults want to nurture and protect it. But what is it, exactly, that needs protection and how best should we nurture children's abilities? What are the consequences of deciding that a child's current performance in a given arena represents an exceptional, innate ability? Is it possible that we use other, unrelated and unwarranted attributes of a child as a proxy for identifying ability? When is exceptional performance in youngsters simply the result of abundant opportunity? And what happens to the performance of those children assumed not to be exceptional?

In this chapter, we explore how the seemingly innocuous effort to identify and nurture ability in children (exceptional or otherwise) often masks a pernicious problem of exclusion and even discrimination. We call this phenomenon the "gap-maker." Problems associated with early identification of ability and exceptionality—gap-making—occur in various arenas. To illustrate, we begin this chapter with a discussion of its presence in children's sports teams. Then, we outline the first part of the gap-maker, early identification, and name its flaws. Later in this book, we extend this discussion by detailing how early talent identification undermines the highly democratic and merit-based ideas associated with the notion of growth mindset.

7

THE PROMISE OF PROMISE

Did you know that a disproportionate number of professional hockey players are born in January, February, and March? These months align roughly with the astrological signs of Capricorn, Aquarius, and Pisces. An assumption from this bit of data might be that the *signs* should be used in identification of top hockey players. Of course, such an assumption would be folly. Even so, the National Hockey League (NHL) appears to be using this strategy in its drafts. Players born under the signs of Capricorn, Aquarius, and Pisces are, in fact, much more likely to be picked up by the NHL. Here's the backstory.

Like most professional sports, players who make it to the NHL have been involved in the sport for many years—typically, since childhood. Often, as youngsters, these players were identified by coaches as having exceptional promise, and they were placed on elite teams. Curiously, multiple studies[2][3][4] have revealed that the young players selected for this distinction by their coaches were typically born in the months of January, February, and March; hence, the connection to astrological signs noted earlier.

Reflection on this phenomenon implies that, rather than identifying promise or talent, the coaches were essentially identifying the most *physically mature* players.[5] Because of a universally accepted cutoff date (December 31/January 1) young players born in January through March, on the whole, tended to be more physically and socially mature than their peers.[6] And so, with the same stroke that identified promise, children born in later months were deemed less promising and, by and large, cut from further opportunity. The phenomenon created by cutoff dates has been labeled the *relative age effect*.[7] After finding that there is a relative age effect in place in the NHL, many researchers continued to study this effect and have verified that it persists.[8][9][10][11]

So back to the ice rink full of very young hockey players. While the hockey coaches were tasked with identifying the most talented players, they unwittingly selected the oldest players. Nevertheless, these early selections were instantiated as meaningful, and expectations and opportunities were set accordingly. Players who mature later, or on time for their age, generally remain in lower-level teams with lowered expectations for their outcomes. Players who were beneficiaries of this special early selection and labeled by their coaches as promising or talented were privy to additional training. Within our current system, such training represents the requisite nurturing that facilitates advancement in the sport and, ultimately, to the big league of the NHL.

TALENT DEVELOPMENT

Okay, this differential treatment could be a problem. But what if creating a gap in opportunity is a part of cultivating talent? In other words, if this tiered system founded on a somewhat arbitrary stratification of players is successful at actually producing talented players, then perhaps the birth month inequities can be forgiven for a greater good. To that end, we need to know whether the system of selecting players at a young age for differential opportunities actually works. That is to say, is finding, creating, or maintaining gaps in opportunity for the sake of advancing achievement an effective method for nurturing and developing talent for professional hockey?

A critical factor in determining if the early identification system works is evaluating the performance of players *once they are in the league.* If Capricorns, Aquarians, and Pisceans have been groomed to become a powerful elite, perhaps it can be argued that the early identification system makes sense given the limitations of any communities' resources. Not everyone can be a professional hockey player, right? If, indeed, this system strengthens the product of professional hockey and creates teams of greater skill, then the early identification system would be validated for attaining its ostensible goal of creating strong players. It would also, to some degree, justify the continuation of the system. But what if these first-quarter-of-the-year players perform no better than others? Or, worse still, what if they perform less well?

A recent study[12] set out to discover who gets drafted into the NHL, how players perform once they are in the league, and how birth quarter relates to that performance. Results were resounding and consistent across multiple controls.[13] The researchers found that, even 30 years after the relative age effect in hockey had been uncovered, players born in the first quarter of the year continue to be drafted into the NHL at considerably higher rates than those born later in the year. In any given year, you can predict that about 35% of the players drafted will be born in the first quarter of the year and 15% of the players drafted will be born in the last quarter of the year.

Even more curious, the data revealed that these same first-quarter players perform *less well* once in the league. The researchers measured productivity by games played and points scored. First-quarter players represent 35% of the league but only 28% of the games played and 25% of the points scored annually.[14] Every other quarter of players (all other birth signs!) outperform the first-quarter players. This is most evident in the performance of the players with late-year birth months (October, November, and December). Approximately 15% of the players drafted into the league were born in the last quarter. These 15% of fourth-quarter birth-month players represent 20% of games played and 18% of the points scored. In other words, proportionally, they accounted for more than their expected amount on these two key indicators of value.

While this might seem like good news for our end-of-year signs—Libra, Scorpio, and Sagittarius, who after all, perform better than anticipated once in the league—the high performance of those who make the league comes at great cost. Consider the many late-year players who were not drafted at all. The opportunity lost for those not drafted is beyond valuation. Moreover, the late-year players who made it into the league were drafted later than they should have been based on performance comparisons. Later draft placement means less money and less opportunity to play.[15] In other words, theirs is a costly battle for recognition and opportunity throughout their years in hockey.

Does the system of early identification benefit the NHL? It is hard to argue that it does. While early identification affords early birth-month players a benefit through higher draft status, the stratified opportunities they enjoyed did not appear to enhance the *actual performance* of these same players. In fact, this system appears to cut the potential pool of resources by focusing on those players born early in the year who quickly establish reputations as talented. This system also puts an undue and enduring burden on players who, during this early identification process, were younger than their peers.

The early identification process confuses maturity with potential to contribute to a team and thwarts opportunity for the vast majority of players. Early identification creates a large gap between players drafted into the NHL based on the time of year they were born (see figure 1.1).

Let's recap our consideration of hockey. A differential system of coaching young children affects the opportunity to play professional hockey. Because the variable correlated with greater opportunity to be drafted into professional hockey—birth quarter—is so obviously not an expected predictor for talent, we pause and, perhaps, wrinkle our noses. We immediately think to ourselves, *that doesn't make sense!* We intuitively understand that some systemic factor, something outside the hockey players' control, *something not about them*, must create this correlation between birth month and draft status. We argue that this factor,[16] the gap-maker, is the *early identification* of players for differential experiences based on perceived levels of talent.

Relative age is the actual story. The cover story is that players are chosen based on merit or promise or talent. Differences in relative age are discussed as differences in talent, and this nomenclature sets the stage for an acceptance of a system that stratifies players. On the one hand, we might balk at implementing a protocol that intentionally and systematically disadvantages entire swaths of players based on the arbitrariness of birth. On the other hand, with the merit-based cover story in place, most people accept the notion that talented players have earned the right to play on an elite team. Those cut, the story goes, just did not demonstrate the *talent*.

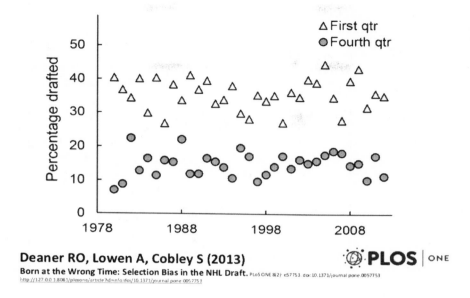

Deaner RO, Lowen A, Cobley S (2013)   ⊘ **PLOS** | ONE

Born at the Wrong Time: Selection Bias in the NHL Draft. PLoS ONE 8(2) e57753. doi:10.1371/journal.pone.0057753

http://127.0.0.1.8061/plosone/article?id=info:doi/10.1371/journal.pone.0057753

Figure 1.1.   The opportunity gap in hockey: Players born January–March are disproportionately drafted into the NHL. This graph demonstrates the gap in percentage of players drafted who were born in the first quarter of the year versus those born in the last quarter. *Source*: Copyright © 2013 Deaner et al.

So the system of tagging *relative-age* differences as *talent* differences creates the justification for the differential experiences of children and allows the continued illusion of a legitimate, merit-based, stratification system. In other words, the adopted practice of disadvantaging players based on birth month has no face-value validity. More likely, the system was put in place for pragmatic reasons, and the eventual consequences may not have been foreseen. The need for the system arises from the idea that identifying talent in the young is a valuable endeavor and that providing talented youth a separate experience is desirable. But this relative age–based talent identification system, while it appears pragmatic, yields less-than-pragmatic results.

THE FLAWED PILLARS OF EARLY IDENTIFICATION

There are at least three structural flaws in a system that relies on the idea that meaningful talent is manifest and identifiable at a very young age. These structural flaws are the assumptions that

   1. talent is (reliably and meaningfully) detectable in the young,

2. talent is innate, and
3. a restricted talent pool is desirable.

These pillars harbor and perpetuate the embedded flaws of miscommunicating the sources of talent, undervaluing the importance of effort, and replacing a diverse environment with an intentionally stratified environment.

Talent Is Detectable in the Young

The first pillar of early identification is the idea that signs of talent can actually be detected in young children and that detecting these signs is a valuable enterprise.[17] In our society children are surrounded with this idea from the time they can talk and comprehend. For example, a child's big sister does not make the soccer team; her brother is a "high" reader; and, later on, this child is herself identified as gifted. The idea that a child's talents can be reliably spotted by adults is often built into their experiences. With hockey, we have an example of a system of differential training that is, at least in part, founded on the idea that *talent is reliably and meaningfully detectable in the young.*

An unwelcome by-product created when acting on pillar 1—that talent is identifiable among the young—is to miscommunicate what talent is and where it comes from. In a classic study on expert performance, Ericsson, Krampe, and Tesch-Romer (1993)[18] found that talent at the highest levels is associated with greater practice time guided by explicit and deliberate feedback. They cite the example of chess players and memory to explain that expert performance is generally domain specific. In other words, chess players have the same *general ability in memory* as their non-chess-playing peers, but the chess player's ability to remember chess board positions, a domain-specific skill, is exceptional when compared to nonchess players. From hours and hours of practice, this specific type of memory is developed. In general, talent is developed over years and years of hard work within a particular domain.

Early identification undercuts the tedious and effortful reality of how human talent develops with practice and instead sends the message that talent is identifiable as a quality, apparent among the select few, and possessed by individuals from the very beginning. In a clear case of actions speaking louder than words, a resounding message is sent from adults to children: *you are either talented and identified as such or you are not talented.* Perhaps not surprisingly, this message is consistent with American perceptions of talent as an essentially innate attribute.[19] As you can imagine, this conception of talent has an impact on one's understanding of the role of effort in talent development, which we address below.

Before leaving the topic of talent, let us be clear: we are not suggesting that there are no innate differences in human beings. Indeed, some people have innate predispositions for developing expertise in given areas. And we concede that there are some children who are clearly positioned early on to excel at certain tasks.[20] But these exceptions cloud the gist of talent development. *In general*, we *all* develop talent through practice and hard work. What we end up being talented at is a fairly direct product of where we spend our time.[21] This is a much more accurate understanding of the relationship between oneself and one's future talents.

Mature talent is not best understood as an attribute identifiable in a young child. Indeed, many of the qualities needed for mature talent, such as a willingness to work long hours or struggle through difficult situations, are not yet manifest in the very young. Mature talent is not the result of a quality perceived in a seven-year-old but is instead the product of years of hard work and focused practice that develops and blossoms over time.

Talent Is Innate

The second pillar of early identification follows directly from the first. We seek to identify talent in the young because *talent is understood as innate*. When a community operates on this belief, it is natural to begin to stratify experiences according to talent. But, if we signal to an individual that talent is identifiable at a young age and imply that talent is an innate characteristic of the child, then what can be made of effort?

A problematic by-product of acting on pillar 2—that talent is innate—is to miscommunicate the role of effort in developing one's abilities and talents. Whereas we understand from research that talent, and indeed eventual levels of performance within certain domains, is developed through years of concerted and meaningful effort, early identification sends quite the opposite message. Remember that talented young children have been identified before they have ever been in a sustained situation that requires effort; therefore, sustained and enduring effort is not likely to be understood as a determining factor for their status. Indeed, over time effort itself becomes not an asset in the minds of many young children but instead a *flaw*. For decades now, it has been understood that children in the United States, taking their cue from adults, see effort as compensating for a lack of ability.

Contrary to the reality that talent is generated from years of effort, we have a general understanding in the United States that effort and talent are *inversely* related. In their extensive research and reporting on the topic of the relationship between effort and perceived ability status, the authors Covington and Omelich (1985) summarized the situation like this: "the potential threat of effort to one's sense of worth increases as the child comes to understand the reciprocal nature of effort and ability status, that is, as high effort in failure comes to imply low ability" (p. 447).[22] In other words, declarations from adults to try harder may be understood not as sound advice but rather as a coded message that one is not talented.[23]

This phenomenon is also manifest in international comparisons of how the sources of talent are culturally understood. In *The Learning Gap*, Stevenson and Stigler investigate cultural beliefs about the source of talent.[24] Generally speaking, Americans identified mathematical talent as consisting of about equal amounts effort and talent.[25] This is consistent with our behaviors. If we believe that innate ability is half of the game, then innate ability warrants attention.

In the Asian countries of Japan and China, studied by Stevenson and Stigler, a strikingly different response pattern is present. In these countries a belief profile emerges that understands effort as more powerful than innate ability as a source of eventual academic ability. This difference in belief about effort translates into different beliefs about the very reliability of early identification. Mothers in Taipei and Minneapolis were asked how early in a child's life one could predict the results of academic achievement tests given at the end of high school. Ten percent (10%) of mothers in Taipei reported that this could be predicted by the end of elementary school compared with 38% of mothers in Minneapolis. This means that mothers in Minneapolis were almost four times as likely to indicate that high school academic achievement performance could be predicted by the end of elementary school.[26]

Consider how this difference in thinking changes things. Where is the incentive to identify innate ability at a young age if it constitutes only a small percentage of what makes someone talented or successful in mathematics? Indeed, there is little incentive to do so. When *effort* is understood as the operational element to developing talent, the role of the adult shifts away from the role of the talent scout. Instead, adults, and the systems they create, logically serve the role of *maximizing effort and opportunity* for all.[27] Talent is developed over time when *large pools of individuals* have access to rigorous opportunities and engage in those opportunities with great and sustained effort.

The cultural belief that *talent is innate* affects our ideas about the potentialities of children. A system of stratification makes sense if ability level is already stamped on children as an attribute and is responsible for a full half of one's eventual level of talent. But a system of stratification makes little sense when talent is understood as the product of sustained effort over time.

A Restricted Talent Pool Is Desirable

The third pillar follows from the second: if talent is substantially an innate characteristic then a *restricted, engaging environment for a selected minority* arguably serves to jump-start young talent through association with other talented peers and is therefore desirable. Seen from the angle that the best players have been selected, this system of identifying talent appears to be merit-based in the sense that the players have earned their spot through superior innate talents and skills and now they can learn on a higher level. The logic follows that these chosen students or players can now engage in learning activities free from the baggage of less-talented peers.

But the flaw of pillar 3 is that early identification *reduces* diversity of all sorts and does not enhance a healthy array of learning opportunities; it diminishes it. Early identification, relying on the idea that talent is manifest at a young age, cuts the actual pool of talent considerably and creates a focused lens on one subset of children. It deprives all children the opportunity to interact with each other and to learn from a variety of peers. It denies the idea that growth comes in spurts. It ignores the reality that children approach tasks in different ways at different developmental stages.

Moreover, if one fourth of children are singled out for the highest class, the elite team, or for gifted status, the pool of human talent has essentially been cut by 75%.[28] While the chosen are surrounded by fellow peers picked for their elite team, classroom, or small-group setting, their work is done within a protected and less rich environment.[29]

Let us consider this specifically within the context of hockey. When we cut players and organize them into strata, we create an environment that diminishes the need for the effort that develops talent. Moreover, the elite players are removed from the growth-inducing complexities involved when playing with teammates currently functioning at a different developmental stage than themselves.[30] At the same time, younger players within the talent pool are now hamstrung by their position in a lower-ranked group.

Effort becomes, to some degree, less consequential for the elite players because the cut players pose little to no threat to the status of the elite, regardless of the efforts of players in either category. Reputations continue to be built based on the reduced pool of competition, and the stratifications become hardened over time. Meanwhile, players and children with latent, unnoticed, or underappreciated characteristics remain in an environment that lacks the same high expectations for future achievement.[31] Thus, the gap in perceived talent; expectations; opportunity; and, ultimately, achievement is created.

Similarly, in the classroom setting, once young students are stratified, their academic-specific opportunities and reputations follow suit. Early identification appears to be a merit-based system wherein adults choose the most talented students. Yet, in fact, early identification is more accurately understood as a privilege-based system that protects some students from the benefits of failure and shields them from healthy interactions among a variety of peers.

Remember that, in hockey, players privileged as elite in youth leagues benefited from higher draft status and then *underperformed* once in the league. As in hockey, early identification in schools eventually affords certain students with a benefit. In this case, the benefit is higher course-taking trajectories.[32] The academic privileges afforded students based on their course-taking trajectories will be further explored in this and later chapters, as will the impact early identification and subsequent stratification have on student performance.

For now, consider that we have reason for concern regarding this system based on the opportunities it denies some children because they are *not* identified for higher classroom status at a young age. Less obvious, however, is the idea that the system of early identification is also problematic because of the performance-enhancing opportunities denied to those who *are* selected as elite. There is less diversity of thought and opportunity for diverse experiences provided in these select settings. Consequently, fewer students with fewer perspectives reach the spots of academic recognition they might otherwise have had to competitively vie for, through concerted effort, as young adults. Instead, in early talent identification contexts, their status has been granted. The stratified environment created by early identification at once bestows privilege and perhaps deflates the performance of this identified and presumably elite minority.

THE STORY OF EARLY IDENTIFICATION

The early identification system is a story that is widely accepted. It goes like this: "Get them while they are young and provide them the special consideration they deserve." Yet this story, that identifying talent in young students and separating them for differential experiences, miscommunicates the source of talent, diminishes the importance of effort, and quite probably affects student development in a negative fashion. The system generated by this story does not create a complex and natural environment for students. It instead reduces diversity of thought, ideas, culture, and experience within this structured environment as well as the pool of children bestowed with high expectations.

In spite of its simple logic, the system of early identification does not provide us with simple and clearly beneficial outcomes. Carol Dweck's mindset research[33] provides a template for understanding the weaknesses of the early identification gap-maker from yet another perspective. We will explore this more in chapter 3. For now, notice that the idea of a growth mindset is sharply undercut by a system that itself is the result of a fixed understanding of talent.

As for talent, we are not denying that some children may be precocious in a given area. Indeed, we are arguing here not for a denial that differences exist between children but for a system that increases the opportunities to develop talent within children to the benefit of all. We argue that looking for differences in young children is much less effective than providing all children with incentives to work hard and nurture the talent they have. Then, in the end, talent has the best chance of surviving into adulthood through the critical act of effortful engagement.

Pick your story: attempt to identify talent at a young age and provide a protected environment for these select children, or develop hard work and effort as a cultural habit in all children through providing opportunity to all. We believe the latter makes sense not just as a democratic ideal but also in the effort to generate talent within our society.

In this first chapter, we have detailed the first part of the gap-maker. It is the belief that early identification is obviously a sensible idea and that acting on this belief is a reasonable and valuable way to organize children. But we ask, once it's been decided to organize children in this way, what happens? What information do we use to make decisions about who gets picked? In the next chapter, we explore this type of professional decision-making across a variety of disciplines.

NOTES

1. Drawing on the work of psychologist Howard Gardner, our use of the term *ability* encompasses and is used interchangeably with various constructs, including, but not limited to, the widely used notions of "intelligence," "skill," and "talent." For us there is no intended or implied hierarchy in relation to complexity, refinement, or otherwise either between or among these various constructs. We will also emphasize the idea of how a student performs in an arena (verb) over the idea of a stable intelligence (noun). Gardner, H. (1983). *Frames of mind: The theory of multiple intelligences.* New York, NY: Basic Books.

2. Barnsley, R. H., Thompson, A. H., & Barnsley, P. E. (1985). Hockey success and birthdate: The relative age effect. *Canadian Association for Health, Physical Education and Recreation, 51*(8), 23–28.

3. Deaner, R. O., Lowen, A., & Cobley, S. (2013). Born at the wrong time: Selection bias in the NHL draft. *PLoS One, 8*(2). doi:10.1371/journal.pone.0057753.

4. Nolan, J. E., & Howell, G. (2010). Hockey success and birthdate: The relative age effect revisited. *International Review for the Sociology of Sport, 45*(4), 507–512. doi:10.1177 /1012690210371560.

5. Malcolm Gladwell (2008) famously explores these implications in his book, *Outliers: The Story of Success.*

6. If a junior league demands that a player must be no more than six years old on December 31, then the player who turns seven on January 1 is admitted to this league along with the player who just turned six on December 31. Considering even the less extreme example by quarters, a player born in late March is still a full half year older than a player born on the first of October. While this seems inconsequential later in life, it is not inconsequential in young children.

7. Barnsley, R. H., Thompson, A. H., & Barnsley, P. E. (1985). Hockey success and birthdate: The relative age effect. *Canadian Association for Health, Physical Education and Recreation, 51*(8), 23–28.

8. Baker, J., & Logan, A. J. (2007). Developmental contexts and sporting success: Birth-date and birthplace effects in National Hockey League draftees 2000–2005. *British Journal of Sports Medicine, 41*(8), 515–517. doi:10.1136/bjsm.2006.033977.

9. Barnsley, R. H., & Thompson, A. H. (1988). Birthdate and success in minor hockey: The key to the NHL. *Canadian Journal of Behavioural Science, 20*(2), 167–176. doi:10.1037/h0079927.

10. Deaner, R. O., Lowen, A., & Cobley, S. (2013). Born at the wrong time: Selection bias in the NHL draft. *PLoS One, 8*(2). doi:10.1371/journal.pone.0057753.

11. Nolan, J. E., & Howell, G. (2010). Hockey success and birthdate: The relative age effect revisited. *International Review of the Sociology of Sport, 45*(4), 507–512. doi:10.1177/1012690210371560.

12. Deaner, R. O., Lowen, A., & Cobley, S. (2013). Born at the wrong time: Selection bias in the NHL draft. *PLoS One, 8*(2). doi:10.1371/journal.pone.0057753.

13. A control in a research study helps to factor out what is and isn't related to certain effects. In particular, the researchers in this study ran their data controlling for draft selection status and player decision to become draft eligible.

14. Thirty-five percent of the players who have been drafted into the NHL from 1978 through 2012 were born in the first quarter (Deaner et al., 2013). For investigation of perfor-mance, Deaner et al. considered only players drafted by 2006 so that the players analyzed had time in the league to meet performance goals, such as games played and points scored.

15. This phenomenon—giving higher draft picks more opportunity to play regardless of actual performance—is well established as real and is called "escalation" in sports circles. See for instance, Keefer (2015).

16. As does Malcolm Gladwell in *Outliers*.

17. Here, we are arguing against the idea that there are highly meaningful indicators of talent that are identifiable among elementary-aged children. It is one thing to notice early that a child has or has not mastered a key learning goal and quite another to think that mastery of that learning goal meaningfully identifies future talent levels in larger and more sophisticated are-nas related to that skill.

18. Ericsson, K. A., Krampe, R. T., & Tesch-Römer, C. (1993). The role of deliberate practice in the acquisition of expert performance. *Psychological Review, 100*(3), 363–406.

19. Holloway, S. D. (1988). Concepts of ability and effort in Japan and the United States. *Review of Educational Research, 58,* 327–345.

20. Chess players, again, provide an example. Bobby Fischer, considered one of the world's best chess players, was a child prodigy whom many adults could accurately see had the markings of a future world champion. But, even here, keep in mind the hours upon hours that Bobby Fischer spent developing his talent. Early signs of talent mean little if not developed.

21. Will Durant (*The Story of Philosophy*, 1926) summarizes Aristotle with the now famous phrase "We are what we repeatedly do. Excellence, then, is not an act, but a habit." Here, we argue similarly that talent/excellence is not an act that can be identified during early stages of development but rather the cumulative result of years of habitual effort toward a complex and mature goal.

22. Covington, M. V., & Omelich, C. L. (1985). Ability and effort valuation among failure-avoiding and failure-accepting students. *Journal of Educational Psychology, 77*(4), 446–459. doi:10.1037/0022-0663.77.4.446; and Covington, M. V., & Omelich, C. L. (1979). It's best to be able and virtuous too: Student and teacher evaluative responses to successful effort. *Journal of Educational Psychology, 71*(5), 688–700. doi:10.1037/0022-0663.71.5.688. Quotes from Covington & Omelich's (1979) further support this point: "The harder persons must work for their successes, the more limited their intellectual gifts will likely be perceived, and contrari-wise, success achieved without much effort will promote an assumption of brilliance" (p. 688); "trying hard causes distress in failure by triggering inferences to low ability" (p. 688); "trying harder causes lowered ability estimates and inferences to low ability" (p. 689); and "students expect others to judge them lower in ability when success is accompanied by high effort" (p. 692).

23. Susan Holloway (1988), in a review of literature on this topic, summarized the research of Covington and Omelich succinctly: "because adults in the U.S. think effort and ability are

inversely related, individuals who try hard are seen as compensating for lack of ability. Thus, adults who suggest to low-achieving youngsters that they can succeed if they try hard may be communicating the notion that the children must make unusual efforts to compensate for insufficient ability" (pp. 328–329).

24.   Stevenson, H. W., & Stigler, J. W. (1992). *The learning gap: Why our schools are failing and what we can learn from Japanese and Chinese education.* New York, NY: Summit Books.

25.   Stevenson and Stigler measured these beliefs in several ways, comparing responses of children and mothers across Japan, China, and the United States. In each condition, the results indicated a clear difference in understanding about the source of eventual success.

26.   Of course, self-report is a notorious thing. But even if these mothers are faking good for the sake of what is expected of them in their culture, this still speaks to the expectations within this culture.

27.   In the highly informative chapter 5, titled Effort and Ability, Stevenson and Stigler report on this phenomenon in great detail in the book *The Learning Gap*. This includes providing historical context dating back to 1893. More on this in chapter 4. Stevenson, H. W., & Stigler, J. W. (1992). *The learning gap: Why our schools are failing and what we can learn from Japanese and Chinese education.* New York, NY: Summit Books.

28.   For the sake of argument, let's say that only one third of that 75% have a competitive chance to perform at the highest level. That still slashes the competition in half. The math looks like this: 25% chosen, 25% not chosen but competitive, and 50% not chosen and not competitive. So, even if we accept that two thirds of those cut deserved to be cut, we have still created a system where literally 50% of the strongest competitors have been cut.

29.   This brings to mind the onslaught of competition created when World Poker Championships were opened to online players. Shortly thereafter, in 2003, the aptly-named-from-birth Chris Moneymaker won the Main Event at the World Series of Poker from the position of amateur online competitor. Without the protection of their elite status as professionals, the professionals were toppled. The next year Greg Raymer also qualified online and went on to win the Main Event. Moneymaker effect. (2018, January 22). Retrieved February 10, 2018, from https://en.wikipedia.org/wiki/Moneymaker_effect.

30.   Consider, for instance, how valuable it might be to learn how to pass to players of varying abilities and skate speed. The complex task of learning to pass while also considering the recipient is more likely to induce growth than if one can rely upon the receiver to accept a pass when sent at the same speed every time. We suggest here that diversity of teammate ability creates a more complex environment that benefits the older or more developed player in unseen and important ways.

31.   The connection between high expectations and performance are well established and documented. See, for instance, Brophy, J. E., & Good, T. L. (1970). Teachers' communication of differential expectations for children's classroom performance: Some behavioral data. *Journal of Educational Psychology, 61*(5), 365–374; Good, T. L. (1987). Two decades of research on teacher expectations: Findings and future directions. *Journal of Teacher Education, 38*(4), 32–47; and McKown, C., & Weinstein, R. S. (2008). Teacher expectations, classroom context, and the achievement gap. *Journal of School Psychology, 46*(3), 235–261.

32.   Think of this as what classes you are on track to take in high school: Do you take Algebra 1 and 2 as your final classes, or do you end up in Trigonometry and Calculus instead?

33.   Dweck, C. S. (2006). *Mindset: The new psychology of success.* New York, NY: Ballantine Books.

Chapter Two

Data Doppels

The Other Side of Gap-Making

In the previous discussion we introduced the concept of *gap-making*, which refers to the idea of systematically offering different opportunities. These different opportunities serve to create long-term advantages (and disadvantages) in performance within any given population. Gap-making contradicts such ideas as *fair play*, *honest competition*, *hard work*, and *merit*. Using the example of hockey, we illustrated how habits regarding the perceived needs of youngsters may deflect attention away from the fundamentally undemocratic, and arguably ineffective, system that has been put in place through early identification of talent. By using the example of youth athletic teams, we showed how gap-making begins (and is maintained) through this seemingly benign activity.

It turns out that gap-making is actually a double-sided phenomenon of which early talent identification is one facet. The other facet involves the selection and use of data sources to inform high-stakes decision-making. In this chapter we explore this second facet of gap-making through examples drawn from medicine, music, and baseball. Then, drawing on our own research, we look at data associated with eighth grade mathematics class placement. Specifically, we explore how students' mathematics placement, similar to outcomes in other arenas, is affected by the use, and misuse, of data.

DATA AND HIGH-STAKES DECISION-MAKING

Let's talk data. In particular, let's look at descriptive data. This type of data describes such things as hair color, heart rate, gender, age, oral reading fluency rate, occupation, width, and the high sputtering clinking sound your car makes when you turn the key. We can use descriptive data to inform. For instance, a mechanic may use the quality of that clink to decide what might be happening in your engine. A seamstress might look at the width of thread to assess whether it is strong enough for a certain pattern. In schools, teachers might use a score on an assessment to determine which students understand a topic and which students need more support, time, and effort.

Now, let's look at what we will call "descriptive-to-predict" data. Often, descriptive data can be used beyond its capacity to describe. If certain characteristics are connected or correlated to certain other characteristics, then we can consider the possible use of this data as descriptive-to-predict. [1] Sometimes, this is very straightforward and, sometimes, not. Sometimes, it is quite useful and, sometimes, not. It might be genetically straightforward that red hair predicts presence of freckles, but is that useful? Being a professional hockey player may help us predict birth month but, while it has been useful to us here, is that straightforward?

Nevertheless, there are times when using descriptive-to-predict data is extremely useful. For instance, while it might not be straightforward that oral reading fluency rate (how *fast* you read) predicts the same student's reading comprehension (what you *understand*), oral reading fluency rate is certainly a useful indicator for a teacher. [2]

At the same time, using descriptive data predictively can get confusing. For instance, oral reading fluency rate provides only information about how fast you read words within a passage. Even though oral reading fluency rate does not provide actual information about the student's reading comprehension, it can help us locate which students are *likely* to need support with reading comprehension because there is a strong correlation between the two. Knowing someone's hair color does not provide actual information about someone's skin, but, if that hair color is red, it does predict that freckles will *likely* be present on that person's skin.

Education researchers sometimes use data to predict one thing, like overall student academic outcomes, based on another thing, say a math assessment taken in middle school. The key here is to notice the use of descriptive data (math score) to predict something else (long-term academic outcome) and to resist conflating the two. Predicting that a student may have poor long-term academic outcomes is not the same thing as describing that student's current level of mathematical performance. But, on the one hand, if we say it enough ("that score means low academic outcome"), it starts to sound like that score tells us more than it actually does about that student right now. [3] On the other hand, we could use that descriptive data merely to inform. We can free it from other duties and allow it to speak simply and directly to that which it measured.

It is important to explore the use of descriptive data, its extended use as descriptive-to-predict data, and how data can be used to either inform or misinform the judgment of decision-makers. This is because, if our understandings are murky, it is easy to cross a line. For instance, we might, wittingly or unwittingly, use an average that describes a set of people to predict the outcome of an individual person. In our examples you will see how professionals use data to evaluate people and thereby make critical decisions that affect outcomes and lives.

We also begin to confront the real quagmire that people do not actually respond to data in the way we might think. Data is quite powerless in the face of stories that contradict it. We will see more of this in chapters 4, 5, and 6, including how neuropsychological evidence stacks up in relation to the informed use of data.

BEWARE THE DATA DOPPEL

Data-driven decision making is a popular idea in the twenty-first century. It means that decisions ought to be made using facts that specifically inform a decision. Do not use what you think is true; use factual data. If we are told that data is used to make a decision, *it seems fair to assume that this data is pertinent to the decision being made.*

But is it that easy? Unfortunately, it is not. For starters, we must beware the "data doppelganger."[4] Data doppelgangers, or data doppels, for short, occur when data or facts that *do not* inform a decision are used *as if they did.* These data doppels can be seen when descriptive data is used as descriptive-to-predict data without the appropriate connection or correlation. Data doppels are the ghost twins of data points that actually inform a decision. Here, we will draw upon three examples of how decision-makers use data to make high-stakes decisions. We look at how data doppels—data that does not legitimately inform the decision being made—arise in different settings. And then, we will turn to our own exploration of this phenomenon within schools.

DECISION-MAKING AND DATA DOPPELS IN ACTION

Heart Attacks and the Goldman Index

In a Chicago emergency department in the 1990s, Brendan Reilly and his colleagues investigated the impact of the decision-making process for determining heart attack risk.[5] In hospitals, heart attack risk is a high-volume concern with a low-volume risk. In other words, many people come to the emergency department with concerns of heart attack but few of those people, generally less than 5%, actually need emergency treatment for heart-related complications.[6] The other 95% of people, who are not in imminent danger of a heart attack, nevertheless place a personnel burden on emergency departments.

For these reasons, efficient identification of patients who need emergency attention (and discharge of those who do not) is critical for the running of an emergency department from the standpoints of performance (*safely* identifying patients in need of care) and cost (*efficiently* discharging patients not at risk). In other words, hospital personnel must quickly evaluate and make predictions about patients based on the data encapsulated in their symptoms and presentation.

After taking charge of this Chicago hospital, Reilly evaluated the performance *safety* and cost *efficiency* indicators with regard to patients at risk for a heart attack. At the time, hospital personnel relied on their experience and the guidance of the attending doctor to order or conduct the tests, blood work, physical exam, and medical history deemed necessary for a given patient. Relying on these various sources of data, the attending physician used her professional judgment to make the call and decide on the level of care needed for each patient.

Next, Reilly and his research team explored the impact of using a heart attack risk protocol that standardizes the descriptive data used to make decisions. This protocol, called the Goldman Index,[7] includes four fundamental points of information: electrocardiogram results, presence of unstable ischemic heart disease,[8] systolic blood pressure below 100,[9] and the presence of rales in the lungs.[10] Because of this standardized protocol, the physician's professional judgment was realigned. Rather than judging which data points should have been gathered for individual patients (social history, physical exam, etc.) and then evaluating what those idiosyncratic data points might predict, the physicians evaluated how the simplified data set fell within a predictive risk factor tree.

So what happened? With the Goldman Index, patients were placed in the appropriate setting with significantly greater *efficiency* without sacrificing *safety*. Recall that the task was to find that low percentage of patients who needed immediate care while also releasing patients who were not in need of immediate cardiac care. In the pre-intervention group, 21% of patients were correctly identified as low risk for heart attack while 36% were correctly identified as low risk in the intervention group.

With the realignment of professional judgment and the standardization of pertinent data points, doctors were able to more efficiently release patients not in need of hospitalization and care for patients at risk for a heart attack. At the same time, performance *safety*—identifying those patients for whom a cardiac complication was imminent—was not compromised. Of the patients who *did* have heart complications within three days of their emergency room visit, 89% were identified in the pre-intervention group, and 94% were identified in the intervention group. [11]

Application of consistent data points and the realignment of professional judgment improved overall outcomes. Perhaps some of the descriptive data previously collected by emergency department doctors were descriptive-to-predict data for *long-term* risk of heart attack but were not predictive regarding the *immediate* risk of heart attack. By using the data that best evaluate real-time patient condition, unwanted data doppels were reduced. [12]

Symphony Orchestras and Blind Auditions

Let's now turn away from the issue of life and death, and toward music. Identifying the best musicians for an orchestra has an entirely different set of contextual factors than those in an emergency department. Whereas doctors are searching for patients in need while ensuring that they do not put any patients at risk, [13] professional symphonies are engaged in the process of locating the most adept musicians whose playing is, literally, music to the ears. A very different enterprise indeed.

Prior to 1970, symphony orchestras in the United States overwhelmingly conducted their auditions face-to-face. That is, auditioning musicians were visible to those evaluating their performance. What impact might that have had on the hiring of women musicians?

In a complex economic analysis of blind auditions, Goldin and Rouse [14] investigated whether the advent of blind [15] auditions affected the increase in women symphony members over time. With the use of nonblind auditions up through the early 1970s, the percentage of women in the most prominent and highly regarded orchestras in the United States was extremely low with none higher than 12%.

Was this low percentage a fact of chance or lesser ability among women? Perhaps their training was not as strong or their commitment compromised? Or was there a climate of prejudice regarding the estimation of women musician's abilities? These were the questions that needed to be explored. And indeed, there is some evidence that prejudicial attitudes may have played a part because there are reports that male conductors openly disparaged the technique of women musicians during that time period. [16]

By the 1990s, however, great changes occurred in the percentage of women in orchestras. For instance, the New York Philharmonic went from close to no women in the 1960s to 35% women by 1996. In 1994 the percentage of women in what is described as the top 24 orchestras was 28%; by 2003 the percentage was 35%. [17] In 2016 over half of the musicians in the top 250 U.S. symphonies were women. [18] What may have contributed to this substantial increase in women orchestra members? As with the emergency department described above, the answer may lie in the reduction of data doppels.

Beginning in the 1970s, symphony orchestras began using blind auditions to varying degrees. Some used this technique for all rounds of auditions, whereas others used it for all but the final round. With blind auditions, evaluators have less descriptive data—they do not see how the players look as they play, and they do not see the gender of the player. Auditory stimulus stands alone.

As Goldin and Rouse report, other factors, besides blind auditions, most certainly contribute to this phenomenon of an increase of women in orchestras. These factors include a democratization in the auditioning process (more people encouraged to audition) and an increase in women musicians in the applicant pool. Changing attitudes, in general, may also have contributed to this increase. Nevertheless, through statistical analyses, Goldin and Rouse concluded that blind auditions have indeed had a large impact on the increase of female musicians hired. Specifically, they concluded that the advent of blind auditions accounted for approximately a third of the increase in women players. [19],[20]

Visual data, although inadvertently a part of the audition process for decades, is clearly neither descriptive nor predictive of musicality itself. Removing the nonmusical, visually descriptive data for musicians lessened the inequities faced by women in their attempts to gain a seat in the orchestra. We can think of these as unconscious, or perhaps conscious, data doppels. In other words, we may not know the thinking or beliefs of the persons making the decisions, but we know that, somehow, gender was used evaluatively in spite of the fact that it is not an informative data point with respect to musicality. In the end, removing the data doppel of gender improved the quality of orchestras because capable, indeed excellent, musicians were no longer being overlooked based on this nonmusical information. [21]

Baseball and Moneyball

With symphonies we see that visual information was used, wittingly or un-wittingly, as evaluative data and thus became a data doppel that decreased opportunity to musicians who did not "look" like they played well enough to gain a seat in the orchestra. Perhaps visual data is more important in a sport, such as baseball. Is it critical to assess an athlete's prowess by virtue of understanding his movement and physique?

Consider the role of the professional baseball scout. Scouts travel great distances to watch high school, college, and young professional players play baseball. Guided by the individual performance statistics of players, scouts then "bring down the blind," so to speak, and engage with the face-to-face evaluation of visual data not captured by performance statistics. We can almost think of this as evaluating the *aesthetics* of a player's individual style. How does the player perform unto himself? What are his qualities? These descriptive data gathered by the scouts are then factored in as the team considers options for whom to choose and whom to cut.

In the book *Moneyball*, Michael Lewis documents a new approach used by the Oakland A's professional baseball team in the early 2000s.[22] This approach to evaluating talent emphasizes the use of descriptive performance data to predict player impact on team results. At the same time, this approach de-emphasizes the aesthetic considerations that can only be understood by observation. In this way, the Moneyball approach simulates, to some degree, a blind audition. Disregard the visuals and listen to the most pertinent statistics connected to the purpose of the organization itself—winning games.

With this new approach, many baseball organizations now value most highly the performance data of a player as the primary tool for locating talent. This approach is called sabermetrics.[23] Similar to the use of the Goldman Index outlined above, baseball professionals still see and are aware of the visual aspects of the people they are evaluating, but the evaluation protocol relies on the objective data points.

Moreover, and again similar to the Goldman Index, which links certain specific data points to risk of heart attack, the data points that are valued in baseball changed as sabermetricians linked certain performance indicators as being most critical to team success. For instance, in the past, hitters were evaluated largely based on their batting averages.[24] But batting average does not provide information about how often the player reaches first base because of nonhitting possibilities, such as a walk, a balk, or being hit by the pitcher.[25] How often a player gets on base, regardless of how he gets there, is called, appropriately enough, on-base percentage.

Furthermore, the goal in baseball is to get all the way around to home plate. On-base percentage does not value the difference between a single, a double, a triple, or a home run. The slugging average of a player accounts for not just a hit but also what kind of hit by counting each base reached toward the player's average.

Because these are the most important things a hitter can do—get on base and get as far around the bases as possible—they become critical data points. Combining the two yields what is now the most highly valued statistic for a batter. It's called *on-base plus slugging*, or OPS.[26]

Similarly, when evaluating pitching, the descriptive data of pitch speed (how fast the ball moves when thrown) has traditionally been highly valued by radar gun–toting scouts. But for sabermetricians, this close-up description of pitch speed is of less concern. The purpose of a starting pitcher is to get players out, to allow very few runs, and to do so for as far into the game as possible. Speed of pitch does not directly predict, describe, or quantify any of these goals. As Lewis puts it in *Moneyball*, "the most important quality in a pitcher was not his brute strength but his ability to deceive" (p. 12).[27]

Without getting lost in the details, one can imagine a visually displeasing pitcher who demonstrates an unusual, perhaps unathletic-looking, pitching style combined with a slow pitching speed. But this same pitcher may have mastered the art of deceiving the batter. This player's talents would be over-looked based on a scout's visual evaluation of performance and pitch speed. At the same time, other pitchers, whose conventional form and high pitch speeds are easily seen and quantified, might easily become overvalued.

Connected to this is the importance of a long history of data. To evaluate a pitcher's worth, teams need as many years as possible to understand the stability of a pitcher's performance over time. For this reason, sabermetricians favor college pitchers over high school phenoms. Again, this is in contrast to tradition where scouts prefer high school pitchers with "brand-new arms" (Lewis, 2004, p. 12) and high-velocity pitches. But the statistics point sabermetricians in a different direction. Over the history of the professional baseball draft, high school pitchers were twice *less* likely than college pitchers to rise from the minor leagues and make it to the major leagues.[28] What was formerly valued (i.e., being a high school player) is now under-stood as disadvantageous. In other words, identifying talent for playing base-ball among the young has not proven to be a winning protocol.

So how did this sabermetric approach pan out? The Oakland A's payroll was among the lowest in the league in the early 2000s. Their players were paid one third the budget of the highest payroll teams. During this time, the Oakland A's accomplished the impressive feat of making the playoffs in 2000, 2002, 2003, and 2006. This success drew attention because it was so unusual to have such success at such a low cost. Sabermetrics is now a widespread approach in professional baseball.

Consider just a few of the many data doppels exposed by sabermetrics. Speed of pitch, while of course not meaningless, can be overvalued. Being a youthful high school player with a fresh arm is also potentially problematic. It looked like an important descriptive characteristic, but it turned out not to be. Even hard descriptive data, such as the batting average, is exposed as a data doppel because the more precise OPS statistic better predicts the player's overall impact on the team.

So, here again, even in a physical enterprise, such as baseball, the reduction of visual data doppels and an increase in precision of the data used allowed the professional decision-makers to better evaluate player performance.

DATA DOPPELS IN SCHOOLS

In the examples previously discussed, we see how data doppels can creep in and be consistently used as if they were suitable for decision-making. At the same time, these data doppels serve to reduce the effectiveness of decision-makers. In all three cases, the professionals making decisions have, in the past, relied heavily on professional judgment and erroneous data points. Considerations such as a person's weight may serve as an explicit data point for a doctor or an implicit one for a baseball scout. But in neither of these cases is that weight data actually critical to the decision being made. It looks like it might matter, but it doesn't.

How are schools and school personnel like doctors, orchestra leaders, and baseball scouts? Doctors have ethical and professional incentives to efficiently identify patients with immediate needs and to safely discharge those without. Orchestras have artistic and economic incentives to select excellent musicians to benefit their sound. Professional baseball personnel have competitive and economic incentives to identify players who will contribute to their team and avoid players who do not. And yet, in all of these cases, we have seen that established systems did not maximize available data and overvalued the "soft" data point of visual information, less informative statistics, or misdirected professional judgment. In these cases, other, less valuable data, such as gender, or pitch speed, or family history of heart disease, stepped in as data doppels that reduced effective outcomes.

Educators have a contractual and ethical mandate to teach the children who attend a given school. Both spoken and unspoken expectations obligate educators to perform their work in a manner that is fair, equitable, and effective. Moreover, educators are expected to do so for the betterment of the community of children they serve and for the individual children who form the community. This, we suggest, is the hope and expectation of the educator.

At the same time, stratified systems of advancement and opportunity have evolved and become deeply entrenched within our schools. These practices are widespread in regard to mathematics. For example, in some cases they are explicit, such as use of different course titles (Standard, Advanced) for the same mathematics content. Whereas in other cases, the stratification system may be implicit, such as different curricular opportunities ("remedial" or "accelerated") within the same classroom. In either case, school personnel have ethical and moral obligations to evaluate whether these systems have educational merit.

Putting aside the merits or demerits of stratifying children for the moment, let's consider that, if a system of stratifying student experience and opportunity *is* adopted for mathematics education, then educators have ethical and moral obligations as well as instructional incentives to accurately identify student performance in mathematics as a means to provide appropriate opportunities. It follows then that a student's access to different mathematical strata should be based on objective, data-driven criteria. Likewise, we would expect these highly academic decisions to be made with (based on directly) descriptive academic data (in this case, mathematical performance data). But recognizing a different scenario playing out in schools, we were prompted to ask, what student data drives mathematics opportunities?

When asked whether they use academic data to determine how students should be placed into math courses or academic intervention services, educators report that they do. Indeed, a statewide evaluation of middle school counselors finds that they report using *both academic and behavioral data* to assist in making placement decisions.[29]

Let's take these one at a time, beginning with behavioral data. We know from many studies that teacher perception of student behavior is racially charged.[30] By this we mean, the race of students has been used in questionable and problematic ways in the context of schools and classroom protocols, including behavior management systems. As you will see in later chapters, because of these clear racial trends when considering issues of "behavior," we do not advocate use of behavioral data as the basis for academic decisions.

Nevertheless, perhaps a pairing of academic and behavioral data can make sense in particular school settings or circumstances. School personnel might make use of these two sources of data to best place students. For example, if academic data is isolated and evaluated carefully by teachers and counselors, then the biases that often surround interpretations of student behavior might be overcome. In other words, when academic performance data takes center stage to evaluate a student's performance, then school personnel might be more inclined to allow the academic descriptors to affect their judgments regarding who is capable of performing at a high level.

We will table this for a bit because, upon investigation, a different problem was quickly exposed. That is, when probed, school personnel reported using *nonacademic* data as a proxy for academic data and to evaluate academic needs. How is this possible?

The At-Risk Model

To answer this question we need to recall the at-risk movement. This recollection helps illuminate the mix-up (or confusion) of using nonacademic data for academic data within the very walls of a school.

Following the publication of "A Nation at Risk: The Imperative for Educational Reform," by the National Commission on Excellence in Education,[31] a movement became popularized that used demographics as predictors of school performance.[32] Descriptive data, such as socioeconomic status (SES), disability status, and race, were used as descriptive-to-predict data for mathematical performance. These descriptive data points were used by many educators to pinpoint which students needed academic support.

Earlier in this chapter we described the use of oral reading fluency rate to locate students who need support with reading comprehension. The process involved isolating a quick and easy descriptive data point to help identify an academic need. The logic for using nonacademic data is similar. Educators use readily available data to narrow the focus and identify student need. Certain children are then deemed at risk for school failure and provided academic support. While expedient in nature, this approach creates a pervasive and lingering problem. Namely, certain demographic characteristics have become conflated with academic ability.[33]

Whereas certain demographic characteristics (e.g., low income and ethnoracial minority status) might predict for realities of low access to particular services and opportunities, the characteristics themselves are not fundamentally related to academic need. Put another way, many difficulties faced by students with at-risk identifiers are appropriately understood as *a product of poverty and/or racialized patterns of inequity and discrimination within schools.* Yet, at-risk status would then be understood and treated as *a cause and an informative data point* for school decision-makers about academics.

The coupling of these factors (e.g., race and academic need) is akin to the correlation we presented in the previous chapter wherein we facetiously proposed that birth month/astrological sign should be used to identify talent in hockey players. In that example, we showed how a serendipitous correlation caused by systemic structure can be interpreted as an identifier for talent. The case of race and academic need, however, is still even slightly different. This is because there is no strong correlation between race, in and of itself, and the need for academic support. Still, many educators use the at-risk factors as if there were.

Using at-risk data for a descriptive-to-predict indicator of academic need results in students with multiple risk factors (e.g., ethnoracial minority and low SES) being identified as at risk and then being provided academic support services. The problem is that all of this occurs *in the absence of an evaluation of their actual academic abilities.* Take a moment to say this three times fast (at-risk need academic support, at-risk need academic support, at-risk need academic support) and you begin to see the habit of mind that becomes the issue. The habit goes like this. Students who do not have certain characteristics (i.e., more affluent, White, and Asian American) are assumed to be stronger in mathematics, whereas those who do have certain characteristics are seen as academically low achieving as a matter of immutable fact and not as a matter backed by academic data.[34]

When asked to describe the specific academic data they use to evaluate student performance, many teachers and counselors describe free or reduced price lunch status, a descriptor for SES, as if it were *academic* data.[35] Moreover, many middle school counselors reported that, because they lacked the demographic data for students' SES, they relied on race as a proxy for SES.

In a stunning case of data doppels, relying on the at-risk model, school personnel reported race and SES as the *academic* data they used to evaluate students and determine class placements.

Perhaps, when policy demands that we use race and SES to find the low-performing, academically at-risk students, it is not a stretch for school personnel to begin to think of these nonacademic data as informative, academic data. In particular, it was clear that being of a non-White, non-Asian race was, for them, an indicator that students had barriers to learning and, therefore, would benefit from counseling services or referrals for academic interventions.[36]

An Imagined Conversation

By understanding students' race and SES as an *academic indicator*, school personnel have not so much freed the data but unhinged it from any meaningful academic framework. Let's stop to consider how this problematic data doppel might play out with an imagined conversation.

Q: Who should be placed in the highest class in math and who should receive support services?

A: The students who have earned the academic right to access these courses or who have demonstrated the need for support.

Q: How do we find these students deserving of higher academic access or in need of support?

A: Use racial group status and free and reduced price lunch status.

Notice that with this model non-academic characteristics are being used to identify academic needs.

The above imaginary conversation demonstrates how the road is paved for well-intended educators to track students by race and SES using the rationale that these factors are legitimate and informative data points for academic decisions. The at-risk model, and its related illogic that the racial achievement gap is *caused by* the poor academic performance of students from particular ethnoracial backgrounds, allows school personnel to "follow this illogic" without consciously understanding that they are segregating students explicitly by race and not by academic performance indicators. Indeed, this illogic is reversed from reality because the achievement gap does not *begin with* poor academic performance (see chapter 4). Mathematics course placement decisions based on demographic information negatively affect—and play a part to *create*—the achievement gap.[37]

Remediation as Elevation

Consider, in particular, the practice of using race and SES as data that informs us about academic ability. Here, a likely *source* of a gap in student achievement—academic placement decisions based on race and SES—is used to assign students to less rigorous or remedial classes in a supposed attempt to narrow the very gap to which these patterns of placement contribute. This is a mighty demonstration of circular logic.

Perhaps the circular nature is more evident with our orchestra example.[38] It would be like using a musician's gender status to identify strength of musical talent. And then, extending the analogy, all but prohibiting women musicians from entering prestigious orchestras and, at the same time, placing many of these women musicians in a remedial violin class as a means to improve the percentage of women in orchestras. Rather than providing them opportunity to attain a higher status, this system would solidify the idea that women musicians are inherently weaker instrumentalists. So, the opportunity to perform at the highest levels is not increased but almost entirely undercut.

DATA DOPPELS IN MATH CLASS

As we consider this circular reasoning and our imagined data conversation, there is one more missing piece of logic. That is, schools, as you might expect, *do* collect academic information on their students. So the obvious question becomes, *Why use an erroneous, and indeed harmful, data doppel when academic data is available?*

For mathematics placement decisions, many school districts have set criteria that *are* substantially based on academic data and explicitly *not* based on SES or racial background. This is, we believe, a self-evident ideal for an academic placement protocol—use academic information for academic placement.

An example of criteria for placement into the top track of sixth grade mathematics in one large and diverse school district is as follows:

> Students must satisfy two of the following three criteria: (a) have a supportive teacher recommendation; (b) score at a high level IV or at level V[39] on the end-of-grade (EOG) assessment; and (c) receive a grade no lower than a 3 (out of 4) on their standards-based report cards, together with two work samples.

The expectation is that, if students meet two of the three academic achievement criteria, they would be recommended for the top track in sixth grade mathematics. This should be the end of the story with students being placed based on their attaining or not attaining these criteria standards.

Unfortunately, the reality of how this plays out is not so clear-cut. We use as an example a representative middle school that we supported and studied for several years. On the record, this middle school used the above placement criteria. In reality, however, the use of data doppels replaced academic data for a large subset of students. In fact, in a recent school year, 103 students (approximately a third of those in the grade level) met the criteria for the highest math class but were not placed into the classes in line with their academic performance. These students were overwhelmingly African American, Hispanic, or from a lower SES. Those who were placed according to their academic performance indicators were overwhelmingly White, Asian American, or of higher socioeconomic backgrounds.[40] We will revisit this school in chapter 5.

For now, notice that sticking to a commitment to use academic data *improves* the chances of African American and Hispanic student admission into the highest rank of classes. Furthermore, this commitment to placing students based on their academic performance leads to continued strong performance by these same students. This is not trivial. Student placement in the highest ranks in middle school mathematics virtually determines the academic and financial outcomes of these students going forward.[41] Middle grades mathematics course placement matters a great deal. These placements virtually determine high school outcomes. Once tracked into different math courses in middle school, high school placements and plans of study are all but locked in.[42]

NATIONAL DATA AND MIDDLE SCHOOL MATHEMATICS PLACEMENT

In light of the locally generated information detailed in the previous section, we decided to look at this phenomenon on a larger scale. We posed this question: Does academic data drive mathematics placement decisions in schools? If academic data drives academic decisions, then we would expect students of different demographic backgrounds to benefit in the same way. We would expect performance to drive placement similarly for all students. In our review of data in a longitudinal national data set that followed students from kindergarten through eighth grade,[43] we did not find this to be the case.[44] Indeed, we found that academic performance in late elementary school was a much stronger predictor for student placement in eighth grade Algebra I for some students than it was for others.

The national data set revealed that Black students' odds of being placed in Algebra I by eighth grade are two thirds that of their like-performing, like-SES White peers.[45] In other words, when controlling for other factors and then comparing odds of placement, a third less Black students end up in Algebra I than would be expected if they were White.[46]

Even more striking is the placement patterns for Black students who have demonstrated high performance. Recall that we wanted to see whether the national data set and our local experiences demonstrated similar patterns of placement. We needed to also look at Black students who had demonstrated levels of high performance as did the middle-school students described above.

What we found was strikingly consistent with our local data. These students have two fifths the odds of being placed in Algebra I by eighth grade compared to their similarly high-performing White peers. These odds play out like this. For every five Black students who would have been placed in Algebra I by eighth grade if they were White, two Black students get that opportunity.[47] Again, this is not two out of five Black students afforded the opportunity; this is *two out of five Black students who are performing at the highest levels in mathematics* afforded the opportunity. What happened to the other three?

Of course, this is difficult to say for sure. Nevertheless, our results imply that the high performance of many Black students is not translating into opportunity in the same way it is for their similarly high-performing White peers.[48] For White students, their high performance can fairly reliably predict that they will end up in Algebra I by the eighth grade. In particular, high-performing White (and Asian American) students[49] generally gain access to the courses for which they are academically prepared. Their performance, more than teacher evaluation, drives their placement.

This is not the case for their Black peers. For Black students, performance and teacher evaluation predict placement similarly. For Black students, performance does not drive their placement outcomes in the same way, and teacher evaluation has essentially the same predictive power as does performance.[50]

HOW SHOULD WE THINK ABOUT THIS?

In our experience, educators struggle to understand their own role in these findings. Many do not see themselves or their own actions as being related to the inequities described by these results. It is important to understand systemic, systematic, and individually driven inputs to these placement inequities so they can be addressed. We will discuss this more in chapters 5 and 6. But for now, suffice it to say that our experience indicates that teachers, indeed people in the United States, in general, have implicit ideas about who is better or not better at math and that these ideas unwittingly affect evaluations of performance. We do not think that teachers and administrators fully understand how powerful these impressions and consequent school placements can be on student outcomes.

Not unlike data doppels that interfere with professionals seeking the best trumpet player, the best baseball player, or the person who needs immediate medical care, our research, both local and national, supports the idea that a student's race and SES become, in effect, data doppels vis-à-vis teacher evaluation of student performance. In sharp contrast to the at-risk approach, we suggest here that skin color and, likewise, SES are not informative for academic decisions and should not be used in the evaluation process. Using race or free and reduced price lunch status as a means to identify mathematical needs and talents is like using gender to determine musicality or weight to determine immediate heart attack risk. It does not belong there. These are data doppels of the worst kind.

The truth is, any objective achievement criteria will increase the number of students in the high tracks in mathematics and *significantly increase the number of students of color and low-income students* as well. The fact of the higher placement will then serve to reduce the gap in achievement, which, as with hockey and birth month, is more correctly understood as *a gap in opportunity*. So, as with orchestras, if a disparity exists among equals, then, once barriers are removed, percentages will shift in favor of the underrepresented population. And, as with baseball and symphony orchestras, when we use metrics that better evaluate students, we will find hidden performers who have been overlooked.

Before we move on, let's pause here to consider the reality that, just as with women musicians, *more* students of color attain higher levels of mathematics placement when strictly evaluative data is used. That might seem counterintuitive to many. After all, the construct of the academic achievement gap has been used to monolithically describe students for several decades. Given the way the gap is framed, it is not a surprise that many people overlook how these averages hide the diverse reality of the performance of all students.

Likewise, many have come to understand or believe that the academic achievement gap is *caused by* poorer ability, which drives an imagined, universally poorer performance of certain students. As discussed above, if the achievement gap is caused by the poorer performance of certain students, then we would need to help them get into higher-level classes with special dispensations. Or we would want to put them in remedial classes to help bring them up to close the gap. According to this logic, using academic data for placement into high-level classes would reduce opportunity for certain students because, supposedly, they are weaker academically and perform more poorly.

Recall the idea of a doctor using a long-term predictor of heart attack risk, perhaps gender or weight, to help evaluate immediate risk. There is a similar phenomenon at play here that muddies the water. It may be true that race or SES predicts long-term outcomes (for a variety of reasons, none of which have to do with mathematical potential), but they do not help us understand individual students in real time. How is a student doing right now? That is what the academic data provides.

Recall also the case of early identification and hockey. When the data doppel of relative age is unwittingly used to evaluate talent, that very factor becomes inextricably connected to current opportunity and eventual affordances. Similarly, when race is used to evaluate performance, either implicitly due to unconscious bias or explicitly in an attempt to find students at risk and in need of remediation, the factor of race becomes tightly connected to opportunity and eventual performance. This would be a serious chicken-and-egg situation, except we know which came first. As with the middle school above, the data continues to tell the story that the data doppels of race and SES drive placement.

Note that we are not arguing here for stratifying students into different levels. Indeed, largely related to arguments made in chapter 1 and here in chapter 2, we prefer a model where stratification is deferred until students are in high school. We also do not recommend that elementary students be stratified based on academic data that, as young students enter school, may tell us more about nonacademic factors, such as academic opportunities within the home or current SES, than about academic potential.

Nevertheless, stratifications are common in the United States. And so it is important to note that the use of objective achievement criteria, stripped of data doppels, will provide more students access to high-quality courses and instruction if stratifications are indeed invoked. Again, more students of color will gain access to higher courses if we stick to strict use of informative academic data to drive decisions. This is important to acknowledge because, given the opportunity, all students, and especially low-income and students of color, will outperform the low-performing labels that have been assigned to them.[51] In this way, using evaluative academic data points for academic decisions is, indeed, a solution within current educational frameworks.

In chapter 4 we will free the data and look visually at this phenomenon of overgeneralizing the meaning of a gap in achievement. We will look to see how the mindset of the gap and the average used to describe it hides individual student information embedded in the data. In chapter 5 we will look at the curious responses that surround this solution in the schools. For now, we want to make it clear that, for all the complex talk about helping underachieving students of color and students who have a lower SES through support mechanisms, teacher workshops on poverty and race, and administrative mandates to meet the needs of all students, there is a simpler solution in our midst. The question is whether we have the will to use it.

As we look further at the solution, roadblocks, and solutions to the road-blocks, let's turn directly to the context of the schools and the people who populate those schools. In chapter 3 we will explore the lived experiences of teachers and students to better understand the human and social complexities of decision-making processes within the schools.

NOTES

1. Keep in mind that, while these predictions can be about predictions for the future (cloud formations predicting tonight's weather), they can also be predictive in real time (predicting whether the same person who has red hair also has freckles).

2. Oral reading fluency rate is an amazing predictor in early education (with a correlation [r] generally equal to about 0.9). This quick and easy data to collect (how many words you can read in a minute) is highly correlated with measures of reading comprehension in that same student. At the same time, with an r of about 0.5, a student's fluency with math facts generally predicts only about 25% of the variance in a measure of that student's mathematical comprehension. In other words, there is a fairly straight line describing the relationship between reading fluency and comprehension.

3. Some people may feel the urge to think about issues of causation. Here, we are considering descriptive student data as it relates to student performance (evaluative) or descriptive student data as it predicts student outcomes (what we are calling descriptive-to-predict data). You will notice that, in the discussion we are having about decision-making in schools, the interpretative hang-ups are not the usual claims to causation. Most people do not think that a middle school math score *causes* poor life outcomes. At the same time, people can come to think of a middle school math score as *describing more than it does*. That current math score is one point in time and describes and evaluates only the present. It does not describe or evaluate the future, yet it can sometimes feel like it does. And this is a different phenomenon than interpreting correlations within the student data to determine what *caused* the student mathematics scores or to think that this math score will *cause* poor life outcomes. If we are not careful about noticing this, we can begin to attach meaning to scores differently to different students or people. More on this throughout this chapter.

4. A doppelganger is literally translated from German to mean "double goer." The term has historically had the connotation that this double goer is a ghost or a twin with an insidious twist. Drawing on this image we use the term "data doppel" to describe something that is used to evaluate but is not actually informative to the decision being made. It is the "ghost twin," so to speak, of data that properly evaluate and inform.

5. Reilly et al. (2002). Impact of a clinical decision rule on hospital triage of patients with suspected acute cardiac ischemia in the emergency department. *JAMA, 288*(3), 342–350. doi:10.1001/jama.288.3.342. You can also find information on Reilly and the Goldman Index in Malcolm Gladwell's (2005) book *Blink: The power of thinking without thinking.* New York, NY: Little, Brown and Company.

6. For instance, of the 1,215 patients followed by Reilly, 44 patients experienced complications within three days of their emergency room visit (3.6%).

7. Named for its creator, Lee Goldman, currently of Columbia University. This is also called the Cardiac Risk Index.

8. Most easily understood as angina, or pain in the chest.

9. The upper number in a blood pressure reading. A systolic reading under 100 is considered hypotensive.

10. Rales are a crinkly or rattling sound indicative of fluid in the lungs.

11. Statistically and practically, this difference is not significant.

12. For greater discussion of possible data doppels in this situation, see chapter 6.

13. And themselves perhaps. When we discuss this phenomenon with colleagues, many wonder whether doctors appreciate a protocol that may protect them from legal responsibility.

Reilly et al. (2002) indicate that no study has been released that documents a stronger identification rate of heart complications than demonstrated in this study using the Goldman Index protocol.

14. Goldin, C., & Rouse, C. (2000). Orchestrating impartiality: The impact of "blind" auditions on female musicians. *American Economic Review, 90*(4), 715–741. doi:10.1257 /aer.90.4.715.

15. Blind auditions involve having a screen so that evaluators cannot see the player. This even includes strategies such as laying down a rug, having women take their shoes off, or having a man walk beside them as they sit down to audition to hide the distinctive sounds of women's heels (Goldin & Rouse, 2000).

16. Goldin, C., & Rouse, C. (2000). Orchestrating impartiality: The impact of "blind" auditions on female musicians. *American Economic Review, 90*(4), 715–741. doi:10.1257 /aer.90.4.715; and Seltzer, G. (1989). *Music matters: The performer and the American Federation of Musicians.* Metuchen, NJ: Scarecrow Press.

17. Wakin, D. J. (2018, April 11). In American orchestras, more women are taking the bow. *New York Times.* Retrieved fromhttps://www.nytimes.com/2005/07/27/arts/in-american -orchestras-more-women-are-taking-the-bow.html.

18. Krauss, M. (2016, July 28). Why more women are winning at symphonies' musical chairs. *Denver Post.* Retrieved fromhttps://www.denverpost.com/2016/07/28/why-more -women-are-winning-at-symphonies-musical-chairs/.

19. They concluded that the increase is in relatively equal parts attributed to blind auditions, increased applicant pool that includes more women, and changing attitudes toward women.

20. A more recent study looked at German orchestras, where the percentage of women remains low at 28%. This study found that blind auditions do have a positive impact on women's chances of being selected to orchestras. The researcher pointed to the initial process of applicant identification as a continued source of inequity. This initial process is not blind and affects the number of women who enter the applicant pool for the blind auditions. See also note 18. Fasang, A. (2006). Recruitment in symphony orchestras: Testing a gender-neutral recruitment process. *Work, Employment and Society, 20*(4), 801–809. doi:10.1177/09500 17006069818.

21. Indeed, blind auditions benefit other underrepresented groups as well by removing the data doppel of race. Blind auditions increased the number of Asians, Pacific Islanders, and Hispanics in symphony orchestras. While Black musicians did not benefit from the blind auditions in the same way, it is thought that this is because of the low admittance of Black students into the most elite music schools. Doeser, J. (2016, September). *Racial/ethnic and gender diversity in the orchestra field.* Retrieved from http://www.ppv.issuelab.org/resources/ 25840/25840.pdf; Wise, B., & Lewin, N. (Writers). (2015). *American orchestras grapple with lack of diversity* [Audio podcast]. Retrieved from https://www.wqxr.org/story/american -orchestras-grapple-diversity/.

22. Lewis, M. (2004). *Moneyball: The art of winning an unfair game.* New York, NY: W. W. Norton & Company.

23. Derived from the Society of American Baseball Research (SABR) and metrics (to measure).

24. A person's batting average is, essentially, his hits (made it safely onto a base by hitting the ball pitched to him) divided by the number of times he tried to get a hit (his at bats).

25. A walk means the pitcher threw four balls (pitches outside the strike zone at which the batter does not swing) to the batter. A balk is when the pitcher begins the pitching motion toward the plate and then stops. Hit by pitcher is just as it sounds. In all three cases the batter is advanced, by rule, to first base.

26. For the uninitiated, let's see how this plays out. Player A gets three singles (three points in 10 at bats), which yields the batting average of .300. Player B gets three singles (three points) and also reaches base on a walk (one point) in 10 at bats, so he has an on-base percentage of .400. Player C has 10 at bats with two singles (two points) and one double (two points) and also reaches base on a walk (one point), for an OPS of .500. Looking at batting average alone, all three players are hitting .300 because they made a *hit* in 30% of their at bats. Certainly Player C contributed more significantly to the team than player A or B, and the OPS statistic accounts

for that contribution. In this way, baseball players who would otherwise be overlooked become worthy of consideration. What we value changes who gets recognized.

27. Lewis, M. (2004). *Moneyball: The art of winning an unfair game.* New York, NY: W. W. Norton & Company.

28. Unlike many other sports, players drafted in baseball do not go directly to the team that drafted them but instead begin their time in the team's minor league system. Generally, players spend many years rising up from Single A baseball through Double A baseball into Triple A baseball before being called up to the actual big league team for which they are drafted.

29. EDSTAR, Inc. (2006). North Carolina's School Counseling Program Review: A State-wide Survey and Comprehensive Assessment. Raleigh, NC: North Carolina Department of Public Instruction.

30. Brown, K. D., Skiba, R. J., & Eckes, S. E. (2009). African American disproportionality in school discipline: The divide between best evidence and legal remedy. *Articles by Maurer Faculty.* Paper 28. Retrieved from http://www.repository.law.indiana.edu/facpub/28; Raible, J., & Irizarry, J. G. (2010). Redirecting the teacher's gaze: Teacher education, youth surveillance and the school-to-prison pipeline. *Teaching and Teacher Education, 26*(5), 1196–1203. doi:10.1016/j.tate.2010.02.006; and Skiba, R. J., Horner, R. H., Chung, C., Rausch, M. K., May, S. L., & Tobin, T. (2011). Race is not neutral: A national investigation of African American and Latino disproportionality in school discipline. *School Psychology Review, 40*(1), 85–107. Retrieved from https://proxying.lib.ncsu.edu/index.php/login?url=https://search-proquest-com.prox.lib.ncsu.edu/docview/860230091?accountid=12725.

31. The argument we present here does not concur or align with any particular major American party. Indeed, educational policy within the past 30 years has generally fallen in line behind increased accountability mandates under both Republican and Democrat administrations.

32. For a discussion of the usage, statistics, and meanings behind this phenomenon see the 2015 article: Kamenetz, A. (2015, April 28). Delinquent. Dropout. At-risk. When words become labels. Retrieved from https://www.npr.org/sections/ed/2015/04/28/399949478/delinquent-dropout-at-risk-whats-in-a-name.

33. Banaji, M. R., & Greenwald, A. G. (2013). *Blindspot: Hidden biases of good people.* New York, NY: Delacorte Press.

34. This is not to say that schools invented this illogical vortex or originated the idea that students from particular racial backgrounds are less (or more) capable academically. What is interesting, and what we explore here throughout, is how these racialized assumptions play out in the data-driven discourse found within the schools.

35. Stiff, L. V., Johnson, J. L., & Akos, P. (2011). Examining what we know for sure: Tracking in middle grades mathematics. In W. Tate, K. King, & C. Rousseau Anderson (Eds.), *Disrupting tradition: Research and practice pathways in mathematics education* (pp. 63–76). Reston, VA: National Council of Teachers of Mathematics. Retrieved from https://www.readpbn.com/pdf/Disrupting-Tradition-Research-and-Practice-Pathways-in-Mathematics-Education-Sample-Pages.pdf (see in particular page 64).

36. EDSTAR, Inc. (2006). North Carolina's School Counseling Program Review: A State-wide Survey and Comprehensive Assessment. Raleigh, NC: North Carolina Department of Public Instruction; Akos, P., Shoffner, M., & Ellis, M. (2007). Mathematics placement and the transition to middle school. *Professional School Counseling, 10*(3), 238–244; and Stiff, L. V., Johnson, J. L., & Akos, P. (2011). Examining what we know for sure: Tracking in middle grades mathematics. In W. Tate, K. King, & C. Rousseau Anderson (Eds.), *Disrupting tradition: Research and practice pathways in mathematics education* (pp. 63–76). Reston, VA: National Council of Teachers of Mathematics. Retrieved from https://www.readpbn.com/pdf/Disrupting-Tradition-Research-and-Practice-Pathways-in-Mathematics-Education-Sample-Pages.pdf.

37. Stiff, L. V., Johnson, J. L., & Akos, P. (2011). Examining what we know for sure: Tracking in middle grades mathematics. In W. Tate, K. King, & C. Rousseau Anderson (Eds.), *Disrupting tradition: Research and practice pathways in mathematics education* (pp. 63–76). Reston, VA: National Council of Teachers of Mathematics. Retrieved from https://www.readpbn.com/pdf/Disrupting-Tradition-Research-and-Practice-Pathways-in-Mathematics

-Education-Sample-Pages.pdf.

38. In hockey, the birth month is an unwitting result of structures in place. As noted above, the thought experiment of using birth month as an indicator of talent doesn't even pass the muster of basic face validity. It obviously makes no sense. Here, with orchestras, personnel often had the explicit belief that women were inferior musicians, so there is evidence that this circular logic actually played a part in the lack of promotion of women musicians.

39. In this district, end-of-grade assessments are on a five-point scale.

40. For other studies on placement disparities, see Hallinan, M. T. (2003). *Ability grouping and student learning.* Brookings Papers on Education Policy. Washington, DC: Brookings Institution Press; Burris, C. C., Heubert, J. P., & Levin, H. M. (2006). Accelerating mathematics achievement using heterogeneous grouping. *American Educational Research Journal, 43*(1), 105–136; and Garrity, D. (2004). Detracking with vigilance: By opening the high-level doors to all, Rockville Centre closes the gap in achievement and diplomas. *School Administration, 61*(7), 24–27.

41. Stiff, L. V., Johnson, J. L., & Akos, P. (2011). Examining what we know for sure: Tracking in middle grades mathematics. In W. F. Tate, K. King, & C. Rousseau Anderson (Eds.), *Disrupting tradition: Research and practice pathways in mathematics education* (pp. 63–75). Reston, VA: National Council of Teachers of Mathematics.

42. Stiff, L. V., & Johnson, J. L. (2011). Mathematical reasoning and sense making begins with the opportunity to learn. In M. E. Strutchens & J. R. Quander (Eds.), *Focus in high school mathematics: Fostering reasoning and sense making for all students* (pp. 85–100). Reston, VA: National Council of Teachers of Mathematics.

43. National Center for Education Statistics, U.S. Department of Education. (2002). *User's manual for the ECLS-K longitudinal kindergarten-first grade public-use data files and electronic codebook.* Retrieved from http://nces.ed.gov/pubsearch/pubsinfo.asp?pubid=2002149.

44. Faulkner, V. N., Stiff, L. V., Marshall, P. L., Nietfeld, J., & Crossland, C. L. (2014). Race and teacher evaluations as predictors of algebra placement. *Journal for Research in Mathematics Education, 45*(3), 288–311.

45. We also controlled for teacher evaluation and special education status.

46. In the study, we used performance in third and fifth grade math assessments found in the ECLS-K as a predictor for placement in Algebra I in the eighth grade. We also looked at teacher ratings of student mathematical performance as well as controlling for other factors, such as SES.

47. These results are consistent with those reported by the Institute of Education Sciences National Center for Education Statistics ECLS-K report from 2010. Here are its conclusions drawing from the same data set: Algebra enrollment was related to prior mathematics ability; higher scores on the ECLS-K mathematics assessment in the fifth grade were associated with higher levels of algebra enrollment by the eighth grade. However, about a quarter of the students who had been in the very highest quintile of fifth grade mathematics scores and about half of the students in the next highest fifth grade quintile had not moved on to an algebra class by the eighth grade. Furthermore, among students in these top two fifth grade mathematics score quintiles, male students and Black students proceeded on to algebra by the eighth grade at lower rates than their counterparts. These findings suggest that some students with relatively strong mathematics skills at the end of elementary school are not in algebra by the eighth grade.

48. There were White students who were not placed according to their performance as well. As we discuss throughout this book, using academic data for academic decisions helps educators make better decisions for *all* students. For instance, students receiving special education services are the most affected by teacher rating and appeared to be placed almost entirely based on teacher rating in spite of performance. Faulkner, V. N., Crossland, C. L., & Stiff, L. V. (2013). Predicting eighth grade algebra placement for students with IEPs. *Exceptional Children, 79*(3), 329–345.

49. While this was not the focus of our study, results indicated that Asian American students have even greater odds of placement into Algebra I courses by eighth grade than White students do. This is most striking when looking at Asian American boys compared to White boys. Asian American male fifth grade students have seven times the odds of being placed in Algebra I than their *similarly performing* White male peers.

50. For more on the experience of Black students, see, for example, Berry, R. Q. III, Thunder, K., & McClain, O. L. (2011). Counter narratives: Examining the mathematics and racial identities of Black boys who are successful with school mathematics. *Journal of African American Males in Education*, 2(1), 10–23; Martin, D. (2000). Mathematics success and failure among African-American youth: The roles of sociohistorical context, community forces, school influence, and individual agency. New York, NY: Routledge; and McGee, E. (2013, February/March). Young, Black, mathematically gifted, and stereotyped. *The High School Journal, 96*(3), 253–263.

51. See, for example, Hoffer, T. B., Rasinski, K. A., & Moore, W. (1995). *Social background differences in high school mathematics and science coursetaking and achievement* (NCES 95-206). National Center for Education Statistics. Washington, DC: U.S. Department of Education; Gutierrez, R. (2000). Advancing African American urban youth in mathematics: Unpacking the success of one math department. *American Journal of Education, 109,* 63–111; The Education Trust–West. (2004). *The A–G curriculum: College-prep? Work-prep? Life prep. Understanding and implementing a rigorous core curriculum for all.* Oakland, CA: Author. Retrieved from https://west.edtrust.org/wp-content/uploads/sites/3/2015/02/College-Prep-Work-Prep-Life-Prep.pdf; Garrity, D. (2004). Detracking with vigilance: By opening the high-level doors to all, Rockville Centre closes the gap in achievement and diplomas. *School Administrator, 61,* 24–27; The Education Trust. (2005). *Gaining traction, gaining ground: How some high schools accelerate learning for struggling students.* Washington, DC: Author. Retrieved from https://edtrust.org/wp-content/uploads/2013/10/GainingTractionGainingGround.pdf; and Burris, C. C., Heubert, J. P., & Levin, H. M. (2006). Accelerating mathematics achievement using heterogeneous grouping. *American Educational Research Journal, 43,* 105–136.

II

Academic Opportunity in Schools

Chapter Three

Diversity in Our Schools

Cultural Preconceptions and Instructional Choices

So far, we have discussed how a phenomenon we call *gap-making* occurs in various social and professional work realms. Using diverse examples, we detailed how judgments that have significant consequences for individuals can be affected inadvertently by hidden bias in decision-making. We then illustrated how the results of those decisions can produce opportunity gaps that have far-reaching negative outcomes, including unfair advantages and unfulfilled potential.

In this chapter, we examine the anatomy of gap-making in schools. We begin with a description of the context of contemporary schools as reflected in the diversity among students. Next, we examine the broad and increasing demand for teacher accountability and its deleterious effects on instructional grouping practices and professional climates in schools. Then, we explore how common classroom protocols coupled with preconceptions about cultural diversity can affect students' opportunities to learn. It is these ingredients that figure prominently in what has come to be known as the academic achievement gap.

MULTIPLE DIMENSIONS OF STUDENT DIVERSITY IN SCHOOLS

If there is one word that best characterizes pre-Kindergarten to twelfth-grade (PK–12) school student populations in the United States today, that word has to be *diverse*. Many education professionals identify diversity among student populations as the single biggest challenge to their effectiveness as classroom teachers, school leaders, or school support services personnel.[1] Demographic shifts in the nation as a whole are reflected in public schools. For example, according to a 2017 report issued by the U.S. Department of Education,

> [b]etween 2000 and 2016, the percentage of the U.S. school-age children who were White decreased from 62 to 52 percent and the percentage who were Black decreased from 15 to 14 percent. In contrast, the percentage of school-age children from other racial/ethnic groups increased: Hispanics, from 16 to 25 percent; Asians, from 3 to 5 percent; and children of [two] or more races, from 2 to 4 percent.[2]

So pronounced is the shift in the ethnoracial makeup of student populations that, increasingly, the phrase "majority-minority" is used to describe the changes. The phrase hints at the projection that "[b]y 2055, the U.S. will not have a single racial or ethnic majority."[3]

The increasing populations of immigrants and refugees in the United States contribute significantly to the growing diversity in schools. In recent years, for example, large numbers of persons from India and China as well as El Salvador, Guatemala, and Honduras[4] have settled in the United States. Others have arrived from the Caribbean, South America, Eastern Europe, the Middle East, and countries in West, Central, and East Africa. School-age offspring of these immigrants, representing the nation's generation of "newest Americans," currently (or soon will) attend the public schools. Irrespective of their immigration status, through school curricula, these children and youth will learn about and be socialized to embrace ideals (e.g., democracy, individual freedoms, justice, and hard work) endemic to mainstream cultural narratives that have been used historically to demarcate U.S. national identity.

In addition to ethnoracial diversity, however, the assortment of languages spoken in today's schools is more varied than in any previous era in public school history. It is distinguished by a wider array of *language families*. This includes diverse dialects that, while spoken by millions of people in various parts of the world, were heretofore largely unknown in most U.S. communities.

Among the vast array of languages (some with multiple dialects) spoken by segments of today's student populations are Arabic, Farsi, French, Haitian Creole, German, Igbo, Kiswahili, Korean, Mandarin, Russian, Samoan, Spanish, Tagalog, Turkish, Urdu, Vietnamese, and Yoruba. Schools in the nation's largest urban centers have long served students from diverse linguistic backgrounds. But today, language diversity has become an important issue in schools serving urban and rural areas alike.

New Normals, Societal Scourges, and Childhoods Lost?

Aside from immigrants, refugees, and multiple languages, other changes in U.S. life and culture have contributed enormously to the diversity we see among today's students. Family composition provides a particularly poignant example.

When compared to previous generations, lower percentages of youngsters know of the legally married, heterosexual couple "nuclear" family arrangement that once was common among all ethnoracial and economic demographic clusters. In its place is a *new normal* that for many students includes a household headed by a single parent, grandparent, or openly acknowledged lesbian or gay parents. Variations on this family composition theme include multigenerational households or those made up of an "extended family" wherein blood relatives and fictive kin share living quarters. [5]

Other new normals vis-à-vis family composition and family life include students who have at least one parent who is incarcerated or students who come from families where one or both parents have been deployed for extended-tour military service. Some students experience variable or transient living arrangements resulting from parental divorce or foster care. Then, there are those whose domicile is a public or private safe-haven shelter that offers protection from domestic violence or homelessness.

A discussion of factors that contribute to diversity in our schools would be incomplete without mention of the impact of social scourges, such as gun violence and drugs, on the experiences of contemporary students. One of the more disturbing realities is that increasing numbers of students know of someone (e.g., self, a classmate, or a neighbor) who has been the victim of gun violence. "Each year, more than 20,000 children and youth under age 20 are killed or injured by firearms in the United States." [6]

Until recently, this particular feature of diversity may have evoked immediate images of ethnoracial minority children and youth living in murky urban enclaves reflecting chronic economic poverty and multiple social ills. Yet some of the worst gun violence in the United States has occurred in schools situated in "nice" locales attended by children and youth from middle and upper economic class White families. [7]

Irrespective of economic background, "[c]hildren exposed to gun violence, whether they are victims, perpetrators, or witnesses, can experience negative psychological effects over the short and long terms." [8] Researchers report such effects as withdrawal, depression, high-risk behaviors, and desensitization to violence. [9] Of course, these effects can (and often do) have a deleterious impact on the experiences of school for these youngsters.

Like gun violence, drug abuse represents still another ominous societal scourge that has become a new normal in the lives of many students. Fatalities resulting from opiate drug abuse, for example, have risen among persons from all geographic and economic class backgrounds. As a result, in 2017, a public health emergency was declared bringing a new level of urgency to the national discourse on drug abuse. [10]

Psychologist David Elkind detailed how some features of diversity, as reflected in changes in family life and U.S. culture broadly, have contributed to kids essentially missing out on childhood. [11] Referred to as *hurrying childhood*, youngsters miss out as they "encounter experiences or are put into situations [in which] they are expected to act and/or reason in ways for which they are maturationally (i.e., physically, cognitively, emotionally) unsuited." [12] Unfortunately, once in schools, some of these same youngsters are robbed of high-quality academic opportunities.

Intersecting Social Axes and Opportunity Gaps for Other People's Children

It is clear that a tremendous amount of diversity can be found among students in today's schools, but less obvious is the *variability within* that diversity. Kids who come from the same ethnic, racial, economic, or language backgrounds can have quite different, if not dissimilar, experiences outside school. But because these axes tend to overlap, important intersections are created that shape and inform the contents of the *academic knapsack* [13] each student brings to school and draws upon in academic learning.

The valuation or importance a teacher places on the contents of the knapsack often varies depending on a number of variables, including students' social identity axes. More importantly, teacher valuations determine students' opportunities to learn.

For example, students who have access to more esteemed contents, such as parents who are actively involved in the school, [14] often receive encouragement, support, and affirmation from teachers and other school professionals. In turn, that affirmation enhances the academic achievement of these students and contributes to the experience of school being perceived and received by these youngsters as relevant, meaningful, and rewarding.

On the other hand, students whose knapsack contains a different, less-valued collection of contents [15] will experience school differently. Typically, the experience will be less welcoming and perhaps even alienating and disaffirming. Teachers and other education professionals may perceive the knapsack contents of such students as substandard, faulty, or even anathema to academic development. In short, these youngsters will need to overcome considerable obstacles to reach their academic potentials.

Serious problems can present when particular social axes are valued over others in schools and when those that receive lesser valuation are assumed to be predictive of a student's intellectual or academic potential. Unfortunately, research suggests that linking particular social identity axes to projections of academic potential figure in the sorting and organizing of students for instruction.[16] Such protocols inform decisions that dictate the outcomes about which students will (and which will not) gain access to particular curricular content.

Teachers and other education professionals respond to the diversity among students in different ways. It is unlikely there is any intentionality to respond unfairly, yet there is tremendous layering within their responses. These layers often represent fault lines or demarcations that inform the substance and quality of the opportunities to learn made available to particular students. For good or ill, the demarcations will align with certain social axes.

Teacher education scholar and MacArthur Fellow, Lisa Delpit used the phrase "other people's children"[17] in reference to the devalued and outsider status often affixed to those students from ethnoracial minority and economically poor backgrounds. Typically, they are the ones affected negatively by what has come to be known as the academic achievement gap.

BEYOND DIVERSITY AND INTO THE ABYSS OF ACCOUNTABILITY

Gap-making in schools is a phenomenon with many facets. Later in this chapter, we will detail how the growing ethnoracial diversity among student populations, in general, and racial minority status, in particular, comprise its most insidious components. For right now, however, we examine how the anatomy of gap-making in schools is traceable to the issue of accountability and demands that teachers *answer for* student academic outcomes.

Accountability mandates, along with the various directives they introduce that shape the work of teachers in schools, rest on the belief that there is an increasing nationwide decline in the academic achievement of PK–12 students. In recent years, for example, widely published results of student performance outcomes on measures such as the *National Assessment of Education Progress* (NAEP) and the *Programme for International Student Assessment* (PISA) seem to offer evidence of academic mediocrity, rather than superiority, among U.S. students. The most publicized outcomes from such assessments typically are reported in the aggregate, thereby obscuring specificities about *whose* children are underachieving. Nevertheless, newsfeeds filled with reports of low performance by U.S. students foment impatience among the public and give rise to serious concern about what and how teachers teach.[18]

Whether the source of a demand for teacher accountability is the local school board, state-level department of public instruction, or nationally elected public officials, along the way it gets entangled in demands for greater efficiency and better stewardship of the funds (that is, taxpayer dollars) that foot the bill for public education. Consequently, the demand for teacher accountability and the follow-up mandates that get enforced in schools and classrooms touch upon myriad issues. One issue accountability demands touch upon, and that is highly implicated in gap-making, is how students are grouped for instruction.

Homogeneous Ability Grouping: The Smoke and Mirrors of Effective Teaching?

The most well-known, if not most controversial, form of grouping for instruction occurs when education professionals mix an objective measure of students' knowledge/skill with a subjective measure of the learning potential of those same students. Commonly referred to as *homogeneous ability grouping*,[19] its aim is to organize for instruction in the same learning space those students whose extant knowledge and skills fall within a particular and narrowly defined range.

This form of grouping is often cited as facilitating ease and efficiency in planning for and delivery of instruction. Yet it rests on the fallacious assumption that learning is best maximized for all students when they are grouped with peers who have the same level of presumed capabilities. Researchers have identified serious shortcomings and even deleterious outcomes associated with homogeneous ability grouping for instruction.[20] Still, the practice is lauded by many classroom teachers, expected by many parents, and persists in schools throughout the United States.

Why, you might ask, is there such a chasm between evidence detailing problems with this form of grouping and its persistent use among school-based educators? The answer can be found, in part, in the threatening realities of teacher *accountability*.

Demands for evidence of student achievement and academic progress represent a *Damocles sword* that metaphorically hangs over the heads of public school professionals, in general, and classroom teachers, in particular. Many teachers feel trapped and profoundly de-professionalized by accountability mandates that dictate what (and, in many cases, how) they must teach. Especially stressing are mandates that require teachers to produce evidence in the form of test scores to demonstrate that their students have acquired particular competencies associated with academic progress.

Assessments used for such purposes carry "high stakes" irrespective of whether they were formulated and designed by local school district psychometricians or international test-making behemoths. The notion of high stakes means that low performance by students on the assessment will result in some form of negative sanction.[21] For teachers, the sanctions can range from personal reprimands from superiors to pay cuts or job dismissals.

Curiously, if you were to poll almost any group of teachers, you'd find that most reject as both unfair and misguided the notion that performance on a single test can provide a complete (or even accurate) indication of student achievement or potential. Rather, most teachers believe a *range of measures and evidence* is necessary to best assess and characterize student learning. Still, accountability mandates typically attach high valuation to formal testing. Consequently, the collegial atmosphere and professional climate in schools during testing periods are often overwrought with tension.

Such school climates cause a level of deskilling among classroom teachers.[22] This means the progressive teaching techniques they may have acquired (through preservice preparation and continuing professional development activities) will atrophy from lack of use. The atrophy occurs as teachers fall prey to a professional culture where there is intense pressure to focus on test preparation and outcomes. An irony surrounds the response some teachers have to such environments.

Experienced and novice classroom teachers alike are often disinclined to adopt pedagogies that research has found to be in alignment with the learning orientations of many students from ethnoracial minority backgrounds.[23] Put differently, in response to accountability mandates, many are reluctant to divert from "traditional" protocols (like homogeneous grouping). This results in long-standing albeit problematic teaching practices becoming more deeply entrenched in the professional culture and climate of many contemporary schools.

Early Identification and Mindset in Grouping for Instruction

Whereas the stress of accountability mandates can adversely affect decisions teachers make about how to group for instruction, other more insidious factors can inform their decisions about *when* to group students for instruction. Early identification of students for assignment to instructional groups presents problems similar to those we detailed in chapter 1 regarding coaches' selections of youngsters for elite sports teams. In addition to early identification, however, the concept of *mindset* complicates issues even further. These two issues, mindset and early identification, feature prominently in how gap-making occurs in schools.

Two types of mindset (growth and fixed) have been identified in research, and both have implications for student success in schools. A *growth mindset* is characterized by the understanding that effort and hard work are the greatest determinants of one's ability to gain success. Conversely, a *fixed mindset* is characterized by the idea that people either are, or are not, good at something. The idea of *fixed* means there is little that can be done to affect the relative level of ability or competence in a given realm that an individual already exhibits. Whether characterized as growth or fixed, mindset affects effort. And effort greatly affects performance.

Researchers have found that the mindsets of children are quite malleable.[24] This means adults with whom they come in contact (i.e., parents, coaches, and teachers) can either develop and nurture growth mindsets in children or create and reinforce fixed mindsets. Early identification of talent or placement in particular instructional groups fits squarely into the fixed mindset framework. Teachers who identify young children as being (or not being) talented or promising at something and, through instructional grouping, provide these children different opportunities based on perceived levels of ability, contribute directly to children's mindsets.

Perceptions and Scapegoats

A well-known adage goes, *perception is everything*. Unfortunately, for teachers, often, it is perception, rather than reality, that fuels sanction-filled demands for accountability. Largely unfounded ideas about what does (or does not) take place in public schools and classrooms can gain easy traction among those who hold the perception that taxpayer dollars are being squandered. Consequently, school professionals are easy targets for critique, evaluation, and even oversight from various special interest groups, influential owners of big businesses, and elected officials.

Often, entities such as these, that are external to schools, issue demands for accountability based on superficial knowledge of the complexities of the day-to-day workings of schools, classrooms, and teaching itself. The power such groups or individuals exercise makes education professionals vulnerable to being saddled with problems that extend beyond the confines and influence of schools.

Classroom teachers experience sharply the sting of being a convenient scapegoat for such entities, particularly during times of real or perceived national crises. A recurring theme at such times is that the nation itself has lost (or is on the brink of losing) its status on critical quality of life axes and its standing among the nations of the world. The culprit in the gloomy prognosis invariably is the low level of student academic progress and the ineffectiveness of U.S. teachers.[25]

For example, the 1983 issuance of *A Nation at Risk*, the open letter to the American people, targeted schools as the dangerously fragile spoke in the wheel of U.S. exceptionalism, global dominance, and military superiority. Warning that the U.S. way of life was threatened by a "rising tide of mediocrity," the U.S. Department of Education Commission members who submitted the report called for increases in academic standards in schools.[26]

Then, in 2001, massive school reform legislation, No Child Left Behind (NCLB), was passed by the U.S. Congress in an effort, ostensibly, to address the long-standing issue of academic achievement gaps. Backed by bipartisan support, NCLB went a step further than its 1983 predecessor in that NCLB made mention of targeted populations (e.g., ethnoracial minorities and students from low-income families) that long had been affected by low-quality schooling. Even so, conspicuously absent from both the open letter and the legislation was sufficient attention to (and calls for) increases in human and material resources needed to significantly increase the likelihood that all students have a fair chance to reach the increased academic standards that were called for so that no child would be victimized by inferior or missed opportunities to learn.

The demand for accountability in schools as linked to high-stakes measurements has created a profound and dangerous vulnerability among education professionals. Significantly, classroom teachers bear the weight of this largely undeserved burden due in part to public perceptions about rampant decreases in academic achievement. In response to the vulnerability, however, some teachers end up making instructional decisions that actually contribute to gap-making in schools. Therefore, we turn now to classrooms and interactions between teachers and students.

GAP-MAKING THROUGH TEACHER DECISION-MAKING

Planning for instruction, executing lessons, and assessing student achievement are well-known components of classroom teaching, yet they constitute only part of the work of teachers. In its totality, high-quality classroom teaching represents complex intellectual activity. Increasingly, as part of their work, teachers are required to find sound solutions to a host of ill-structured problems[27] that affect student learning both directly and indirectly.

The multidimensional diversity among student populations that we described earlier in this chapter adds to the complexity of classroom teaching. This means that, in addition to having in-depth content knowledge and high-quality instructional skills, teachers now need to acquire (and draw upon) knowledge of differing worldviews, value orientations, beliefs, attitudes, assumptions, and experiences—in a phrase, the diverse *cultural backgrounds* of their students.[28] Another way to think of this is, in today's highly diverse school settings, teachers need cross-cultural intelligence to interact with individual students and draw upon and build the benefits of a diverse environment.[29]

On the whole, teachers exercise considerable autonomy within their individual classrooms and have substantial power over the students they are assigned to teach. In a typical school day, teachers make hundreds of decisions that either involve or affect their students. These decisions touch upon myriads of topics ranging from the mundane to the critical. Yet, among the most consequential decisions teachers make are those that inform students' opportunities to learn and the sophistication of the content students are likely to encounter. Such decisions can affect students' lives in ways that extend far beyond the classroom.

Cultural Difference as a Factor in Teachers' Decision-Making

Like their students, teachers too are cultural beings. This means teachers' cultural backgrounds inform how they enact the various aspects of their professional roles as teachers. It also means that the worldviews, value orientations, and beliefs that teachers live by outside of school will inform (if not dictate) the various ways they engage with, and make decisions about, the students they teach inside schools.

Today, it is commonplace for the backgrounds of teachers (e.g., cultural, ethnoracial, economic, and experiential) to differ considerably from those of a high percentage of the students they are assigned to teach. For example, table 3.1 reveals that the ethnoracial background of the majority of teachers in U.S. public schools is quite dissimilar to that of the students they teach.[30]

How teachers perceive and receive students whose backgrounds differ from theirs is of considerable relevance to a discussion about gap-making. This is because, although there are many factors that enter into how teachers make decisions in schools, arguably the most insidious is the ethnoracial backgrounds of their students. Studies suggest the race of students, for example, is an especially influential factor in teacher decision-making in regard to behavior management and discipline of students.

A 2014 report from the Department of Education illustrated how students of color in public schools are more likely to be suspended and receive referrals to law enforcement. In fact, at all age levels, [B]lack children are three times as likely as [W]hite children to face suspensions. These hold even for the young-

Group	White Non-Hispanic	Black Non-Hispanic	Hispanic Any race	Asian Non-Hispanic	Pacific Islander	American Indian/ Alaska Native	Two or more races
Teachers	80.1	6.7	8.8	2.3	0.2	0.4	1.4
Students	50	16	25	5		1	3

Table 3.1.   **Percentages of Public School Teachers and Students by Race/Ethnicity** *Source*: **National Center for Education Statistics. IES (Table 209.10.) Latest year available 2015–2016; Musu-Gillette, L., deBrey, C., McFarland, J., Hussar, W., and Wilkinson-Flicker, S. (2017).** *Status and trends in the education of racial and ethnic groups 2017* **(NCES 2017-051). U.S. Department of Education, National Center for Education Statistics. Washington, D.C. Retrieved October 18, 2018 from http://nces.ed.gov/pubsearch.**

est students. At the preschool levels, [B]lack students represent 18 percent of enrollment but 48 percent of suspensions. Further while boys receive the majority of suspensions, African American girls receive suspensions at a higher rate—approximately 12 percent—than girls of any other backgrounds.[31]

Bias in how students are disciplined in schools has long been considered a highly problematic feature of how race operates in teachers' decision-making. Such bias affects negatively how students see themselves as well as how they are perceived by their peers.

Also, racial bias in how student behavior is managed or how teachers enforce discipline protocols can directly affect opportunities to learn. Students who are suspended or otherwise extracted from the classroom setting cannot learn because they are not present to be taught. But even more onerous than race bias in behavior management and discipline protocols is when race is implicated in how teachers make decisions about the placement of students for instruction.

Teacher Preconceptions: Critical Indicators of Student Learning Potential?

The sheer power teachers exercise in their classrooms and interactions with students is most evident (and consequential) when teachers opine about the learning potential of students. Student placement for instruction, whether intended to offer acceleration, remediation, or individualized instruction, typically is initiated by teacher recommendation based on that same teacher's *perceptions* of the student's talent, capabilities, and academic potential.

A profoundly troubling issue presents in the teaching-learning process, however, when teachers' perceptions are grounded in and informed by preconceptions, stereotypes,[32] and biased assumptions based on students' cultures, social circumstances, or ethnoracial backgrounds. It seems fair to say that all teachers love students and they could scarcely imagine the possibility (not to mention probability) that, as a teacher, they would exhibit prejudice or racism toward their students. Yet, research indicates that unintentional biases can and do infiltrate and affect cross-racial interactions.[33] Such is the case even between teachers and students.

Recall from chapter 2 that our research investigates the role of *teacher ratings* of student mathematics performance versus students' demonstrated mathematics performance. Specifically, we examined how elementary school teacher ratings and elementary school student mathematics performance predicted placement in algebra by eighth grade. Using a national data set[34] to compare these factors against mathematics class placement in eighth grade, we found that the impact of these two factors (i.e., teacher rating of student versus demonstrated student mathematical performance) played out dissimilarly for different sets of students.

What is striking here is that the *actual mathematical performance* of high-achieving Black students *was not* as strong a predictor of how they were placed for instruction as was actual mathematics performance in the placement for White students. This implies that the actual performance in mathematics did not have the same leverage for some students as it did for others. When we analyzed the data from a different perspective, our results indicated that high-performing Black students had two fifths the odds of being placed in algebra by the eighth grade compared to their high-performing White peers.[35]

The chilling results of our findings have led us to question the extent to which teachers' own preconceptions served as an implicit data point, a *data doppel*, in determining how particular children were placed for instruction subsequent to their elementary school experience. Instead of allowing objective data (students' actual performance ratings) to inform recommendations for how students were placed for instruction, it appears that other subjective data—that is, teachers' own preconceptions about students' learning potential—represented the driving force that informed how students were placed for instruction.

Moreover, because the power/influence of teacher preconception over actual student performance was more striking for Black students, it suggests that the *race* of the students had a more significant, albeit negative, impact on their opportunities to learn than their actual demonstrated abilities. The odds for high-performing Black students to be placed in algebra by eighth grade were not significantly better than their low-performing same-race peers.

HETEROGENEOUS GROUPS AND GROWTH MINDSET: TOWARD NEUTRALIZING PROBLEMATIC DECISION-MAKING

The insidious influence of subjective data doppels on student assignment for instruction stands in stark contrast to grouping practices that provide access to rigorous instructional opportunities for all children regardless of their current levels of performance or their immutable characteristics, such as race. We believe a different orientation to instructional grouping along with deliberate promotion of a growth mindset has the potential to neutralize cultural preconceptions and the negative biases in teacher decision-making they engender. In schools where the former has been instituted, the practice is called "heterogeneous grouping."[36]

By virtue of providing all students the opportunity to learn all material, heterogeneous grouping sends a growth mindset message. Consistently, research findings have demonstrated that students with a growth mindset are positioned to better develop their talents over their peers with fixed mindsets.[37] For example, a study of middle school students found that those who held a growth mindset showed increasing mathematics scores at each of four testing points throughout seventh and eighth grades, compared to stagnant scores for those with fixed mindsets.

Likewise, another study that reviewed the work of over 168,000 tenth grade Chilean students (approximately three quarters of the 10th grade population) found that students with a growth mindset scored better on the mathematics and language national standardized tests.[38] In fact, students with a growth mindset and family income in the lowest 10% of the country (often a strong indicator of weak academic performance) scored as well as students with fixed mindsets and family incomes in the 80th percentile, families with incomes approximately 13 times greater.

A study of Greek high school students sought to explain why a growth mindset leads to higher academic achievement. It showed that the presence of a growth mindset led to student-reported increased studying and decreased procrastination (which in turn led to higher grades) compared to those with a fixed mindset.[39] Then (beyond the impacts of schooling), another study found that not only do middle schoolers with a growth mindset related to intelligence show increased grades and placement in higher-level mathematics classes, but similar beliefs about their emotions (that they can be changed or improved) led to increased well-being, particularly in those who originally reported low well-being.[40]

It seems obvious that it is difficult to send the growth mindset message within the context of a fixed system, such as homogeneous grouping. Also, growth mindset cannot take root in classroom environments where learning opportunities for students are based (either exclusively or mainly) on teachers' *perceptions* of students' abilities and academic potentials.

TROUBLING STRATIFICATION

Grouping policies in U.S. schools are often grounded in a fixed mindset wherein students are grouped for instruction with those assumed to share their talents. This can, and often does, start as early as kindergarten when, based on their perceived abilities, teachers organize students into different groups for instruction. It also starts when students are assigned to different classrooms with different teachers and the aim is to provide different (more or less challenging) curricular content.

Such stratification systems in schools are deeply entrenched by second or third grade, when teachers begin to identify some children as gifted[41] while others are identified (and treated) as average or even below average. These within-class and within-school differentiations are further solidified at the sixth grade level. Worse still, there is evidence to suggest that the differentiations are greatly informed by immutable (race and ethnicity) and status (economic class) characteristics of the students themselves.

Using mathematics instruction as our example, our research considered the role of stratification as it relates to future outcomes in mathematics placement. Between fifth and sixth grades, educators make decisions about student outcomes by providing either explicitly different content or content that is taught at a substantively different pace to different strata of students. Once stratified in sixth grade, students' opportunities to learn mathematics in subsequent grades have already been determined. Overwhelmingly, research shows that the students who do not study algebra by eighth grade do not enroll in upper-level mathematics once they enter high school.[42] For at least some students, rather than an absence of talent or the presence of low learning potential determining their fate, it was a faulty decision by their teachers that was used to set this tragic outcome into motion. Put another way, the presence of high performance may not be enough for Black and Hispanic students to overcome the faulty decision-making processes and systemic validation of those processes that serve to diminish the opportunities and prospects of these students.

In the next chapter, we continue our exploration of academic opportunity within schools. We do this by examining disconnections between student performance, student opportunity, and student outcomes. We acknowledge the complexity of using data to identify students for academic opportunity within a cultural context that demonstrates an urge to stratify students. In particular, we consider what data can tell us about ourselves, our systems, and our students.

NOTES

1. We use "diversity" in a *descriptive* sense and in reference to variations among student populations along various social axes, including (but not limited to) race, ethnicity, economic class, primary language, religion, and so on. The complex intellectual activity that is classroom teaching is intensified in school and classroom environments that are diverse. Even so, we acknowledge from our work in public schools the troubling use of the term "diversity" in an *evaluative* sense. For some, diversity is a euphemism intended to soften or even disguise negative perceptions of particular social axes variations among student populations. In short, we've experienced situations where the phrase "student diversity" served as a code word used among education professionals in reference to those youngsters (typically from ethnoracial minority backgrounds) whose very presence in schools is perceived as introducing extreme negative challenges to the teaching process.

2. Musu-Gillette, L., de Brey, C., McFarland, J., Hussar, W., Sonnenberg, W., & Wilkinson-Flicker, S. (2017). *Status and trends in the education of racial and ethnic groups 2017* (NCES 2017-051). National Center for Education Statistics. Washington, DC: U.S. Department of Education, p. 8.

3. Cohn, D., & Caumont, A. (2016, March 31). *10 demographic trends that are shaping the U.S. and the world.* Retrieved from http://www.pewresearch.org/fact-tank/2016/03/31/10-demographic-trends-that-are-shaping-the-u-s-and-the-world/. Ostensibly, the term means that students from ethnoracial "minority" groups form the majority of a school/district population.

However, no corollary phrase (e.g., "diminishing majority") has been coined (or used widely) to characterize the declining population of White students. Indeed, the term "minority" typically is not linked to White student populations even in so-called majority-minority districts. Thus, the oxymoronic form of the phrase majority-minority reveals that, in the realm of schooling, the notion of minority seems to have been permanently linked to certain segments of the population while majority status seems permanently associated with racial Whiteness. This makes obvious that as stand-alone concepts, "majority" and "minority" are imbued with sociopolitical meaning and connotation that reach beyond the actual numeric composition of any given ethnoracial population in a school district.

4. Zong, J., & Batalova, J. (2017). *Chinese immigrants in the United States.* https://www.migrationpolicy.org/article/chinese-immigrants-united-states; and Pew Research Center. (2017). *Hispanic trends.* Retrieved from http://mailchi.mp/pewresearch/w8zd23u60n-2570173?e=b3bf5af499.

5. "In 2014, across racial/ethnic groups, the majority of children under age 18 lived with married parents, with the exception of Black and American Indian/Alaska Native children. A higher percentage of Asian children (82 percent) lived with married parents than the percentage of White children (73 percent), Pacific Islander children (65 percent), Hispanic children and children of [t]wo or more races (56 percent each), American Indian/Alaska Native children (43 percent), and Black children (33 percent) who lived with married parents. The percentage of children living with a female parent with no spouse present was highest for Black children (57 percent), followed by children who were American Indian/Alaska Native (39 percent), of [t]wo or more races (34 percent), Hispanic (32 percent), Pacific Islander (25 percent), White (18 percent), and Asian (12 percent). . . . The percentage of children living with a male parent with no spouse present was higher for American Indian/Alaska Native children (14 percent) than the percentages of children of all other racial/ethnic groups; conversely, the percentage of Asian children living with a male parent with no spouse present (5 percent) was lower than the percentages of children of all other racial/ethnic groups" (Musu-Gillette et al., 2017, p. 16).

6. Reich, K., Culross, P. L., & Behrman R. E. (2002). Children, youth, and gun violence: Analysis and recommendations. *The Future of Children, 12*(2), 5.

7. The barrage of school shootings that have radically altered American's perceptions of violence in schools began in 1999 at Columbine High School in Colorado, which resulted in 15 deaths. Others that have contributed to the new perception of school violence include 27 killed in the 2012 shootings at Sandy Hook Elementary School in Newtown, Connecticut, and in 2018 when 17 were killed in a shooting at Marjory Stoneman Douglas High School in Parkland, Florida. Each of these mass murders has resulted in a re-visitation of gun laws in the United States, an issue that is decidedly politically controversial.

8. Reich, K., Culross, P. L., & Behrman R. E. (2002). Children, youth, and gun violence: Analysis and recommendations. *The Future of Children, 12*(2), 11.

9. Garbarino, J., Bradshaw, C. P., & Vorrasi, J. A. (2002). Mitigating the effects of gun violence on children and youth. *The Future of Children, 12*(2), 72–85.

10. This response contrasts sharply with that of the 1980s when the rapid spread of crack cocaine sale and usage decimated many urban communities populated by economically poor and ethnoracial minority peoples. See, for example, Alexander, M. (2012). *The new Jim Crow: Mass incarceration in the age of colorblindness.* New York, NY: The New Press. Different from previous eras, the public reaction to contemporary drug abuse includes calls for cessation treatment and mental-health counseling. This more compassionate response has gained widespread backing from citizens and politicians alike. See Tiger, R. (2017). Race, class, and the framing of drug epidemics. *Contexts, 16*(4), 46–51. We believe this new emphasis on support and rehabilitation (rather than punishment and incarceration) for drug abuse sufferers is a far better and morally defensible response to this great societal ill.

11. See Elkind, D. (2001). *The hurried child: Growing up too fast too soon.* Cambridge, MA: Perseus Publishers. Herein, he describes how shifting of responsibilities and expectations to youngsters, as well as youngsters being situated prematurely in circumstances and encounters that traditionally were associated with (or reserved for) adulthood, has contributed to a loss of childhood.

12. Marshall, P. L. (2002). *Cultural diversity in our schools*. Belmont, CA: Wadsworth Publishing, p. 263.

13. The *knapsack* metaphor is used here in a way not dissimilar to its use by women's studies scholar Peggy McIntosh (1988) in her now germinal work, *White Privilege and Male Privilege: A Personal Account of Coming to See Correspondences through Work in Women's Studies*. McIntosh likened the knapsack of White privilege to "invisible . . . special provisions, assurances, tools, maps, guides, codebooks, passports, visas, clothes, compass, emergency gear, and blank checks" (pp. 56–57). For students in schools, the contents of the academic knapsack can be conceived similarly with the addition of human and material resources that are accessible (or inaccessible) based on the economic and social status of their adult caregivers.

14. Valued contents can include middle class status where a student's parents are active in the school and responsive to teacher's communications. Other valued contents can include a student's facility with standard/academic English, heterosexual orientation, and out-of-school or home-life experiences that align with the emphases of traditional curricular content, instructional strategies, interpersonal protocols, and so on.

15. These may include personal presentation as reflected in manner of dress, hairstyle, interpersonal interactions/comportment, and speech patterns. Also, immutable characteristics that have been found to receive lower valuation in schools have included darker skin color, homosexual presentation, and physical disability. See Irvine, J. J. (1991). *Black students and school failure*. New York, NY: Praeger; Griffin, P., & Ouellett, M. (2003). From silence to safety and beyond: Historical trends in addressing lesbian, gay, bisexual, transgender issues in K–12 schools. *Equity & Excellence in Education, 36,* 106–114; and Murray, O. (2011). Queer youth in heterosexist schools: Isolation, prejudice and no clear supportive policy frameworks. *Multicultural Perspectives, 13*(4), 215–219.

16. Faulkner, V. N., Stiff, L. V., Marshall, P. L., Nietfeld, J., & Crossland, C. L. (2014). Race and teacher evaluations as predictors of algebra placement. *Journal for Research in Mathematics Education, 45*(3), 288–311.

17. This phrase was introduced to teacher education discourse during the "literacy wars" of the late 1980s and the debates over *process-oriented* (whole language) versus *skills-based* (phonics) approaches to early reading/literacy instruction. See Delpit, L. (1988). The silenced dialogue: Power and pedagogy in educating other people's children. *Harvard Educational Review, 58*(3), 280–298. Therein, Delpit brought to the forefront the critical urgency of providing high-quality foundational literacy instruction for African American youngsters. The phrase "other people's children" refers to those youngsters (typically from ethnoracial minority and economically poor family backgrounds) who, by virtue of their group social status, must learn rules and protocols in schools associated with the dominant White middle class group to successfully navigate academic (and societal) spaces where their own cultural capital has long been pathologized, devalued, negated, or ignored outright. Also see Delpit, L. (2012). *Multiplication is for White people: Raising expectations for other people's children*. New York: The New Press.

18. Though beyond the scope of this book, findings of Lubienski and Lubienski indicate that public school children are, indeed, outperforming private school children in mathematics. Also consider that U.S. students' NAEP scores in mathematics have continued to rise. So, while U.S. students are decidedly not where they should be by many metrics of student performance and equity, there are indications that educators in public schools are working to address the issues that are raised, such as that of improving mathematical instruction. Lubienski, C., & Lubienski, S. T. (2014). *The public school advantage: Why public schools outperform private schools*. Chicago, IL: University of Chicago Press.

19. Another common term for this form of grouping is "academic tracking." Although homogeneous grouping technically can be used to organize students for temporary/short-term instruction purposes (i.e., grouping directed at, say, a finite series of lessons related to a particular skill), the idea of academic tracking typically has been used to define a youngster's entire schooling experience and, ultimately, the youngster's life chances beyond school. As such, tracking has the chilling effect of foreclosing learning possibilities and opportunities that extend beyond those specifically defined as consistent with the particular track (e.g., vocational, technical, or academic) to which the student has been assigned.

20. Oakes, J. (2005). *Keeping track.* New Haven, CT: Yale University Press.

21. For their part, students may face sanctions that require them to attend extra class sessions, repeat a class, or be retained at a given grade level.

22. Apple, M. W., & Jungck, S. (1990). You don't have to be a teacher to teach this unit: Teaching, technology, and gender in the classroom. *American Educational Research Journal, 27*(2), 227–251.

23. This includes pedagogical orientations that are culturally responsive and culturally restorative and have been found to promote school interest and higher academic achievement results among students. A growing body of scholarship and research across varying fields and curricular content areas, including mathematics and science, has demonstrated that, when the content, teaching strategies, and interpersonal protocols in classrooms are in alignment with the cultural backgrounds of students, academic achievement is enhanced significantly. See, for example, Gutstein, E., Lipman, P., Hernadez, P., & de los Reyes, R. (1997). Culturally relevant mathematics teaching in a Mexican American context. *Journal for Research in Mathematics Education, 28*(6), 709–737; Ladson-Billings, G. (1997). It doesn't add up: African American students' mathematics achievement. *Journal for Research in Mathematics Education, 28*(6), 697–708; Martin, D. B. (2000). *Mathematics success and failure among African-American youth: The roles of sociohistorical context, community forces, school influence, and individual agency.* Mahwah, NJ: Lawrence Erlbaum Associates; and Nasir, N. S., Hand, V., & Taylor, E. V. (2008). Culture and mathematics in school: Boundaries between "cultural" and "domain" knowledge in the mathematics classroom and beyond. *Review of Research in Education, 32,* 187–240.

24. Dweck, C. S. (2006). *Mindset: The new psychology of success.* New York, NY: Ballantine Books.

25. The 1960s decade subsequent to the launching of the Soviet Satellite *Sputnik* resulted in a plethora of critiques of teachers and U.S. schools. See, for example, Conant, J. B. (1963). *The education of American teachers.* New York: McGraw-Hill Book Co., Inc.; Koerner, J. D. (1963). *The miseducation of American teachers.* Boston, MA: Houghton Mifflin; and Rickover, H. G. (1963). *American education, a national failure: The problem of our schools and what we can learn from England.* New York, NY: E.P. Dutton & Co.

26. See National Commission on Excellence in Education. (1983). *A nation at risk: The imperative for educational reform.* Washington, DC: U.S. Department of Education.

27. Kitchener and King (1990) noted that "ill-structured" or real-world problems have multiple dimensions and "all the parameters are seldom clear or available [thus making it] . . . difficult to determine when and whether an adequate solution has been identified" (p. 164). Similarly, solutions for ill-structured problems are often "based on incomplete information or evidence that is subject to multiple interpretations" (King & Kitchener, 2002, p. 56). See King, P. M., & Kitchener, K. S. (2002). The reflective judgment model: Twenty years of research on epistemic cognition. In B. K. Hofer and P. R. Pintrich (Eds.), *Personal epistemology: The psychology of beliefs about knowledge and knowing* (pp. 37–61). Mahwah, NJ: Lawrence Erlbaum & Associates; and Kitchener, K. S., & King, P. M. (1990). The reflective judgment model: Transforming assumptions about knowing. In J. Mezirow & Associates (Ed.), *Fostering critical reflection in adults: A guide to transformative and emancipatory learning* (pp. 159–176). San Francisco, CA: Jossey-Bass.

28. A growing body of empirical evidence indicates that teachers who are most knowledgeable about the backgrounds of their students and the larger sociopolitical context in which schooling occurs are more successful in teaching today's diverse students. See Ladson-Billings, G. (1994). *The dreamkeepers: Successful teachers of African American students.* San Francisco, CA: Jossey-Bass.

29. Moreover, as referenced in chapter 2, teachers need to notice how their own cultural assumptions affect their valuation of students. Teachers also need to become aware of and critique tendencies to bond with those whose social cues they understand (through their own socialization) as they strive to evaluate fairly the needs of all their students.

30. See, for example, Sleeter, C. E. (2001). Preparing teachers for culturally diverse schools: Research and the overwhelming presence of whiteness. *Journal of Teacher Education, 52*(2), 94–106. Various teacher education scholars have examined the paucity of teacher candidates of

color and the dominance of White, middle class teacher candidates in teacher education programs throughout the United States. For additional discussion, see Zumwalt, K., & Craig, E. (2008). Who is teaching? Does it matter? In M. Cochran-Smith, S. Feiman-Nemser, D. J. McIntyre, & K. E. Demers (Eds.), *Handbook of research on teacher education: Enduring questions in changing contexts* (3rd ed., pp. 134–156). New York, NY: Routledge.

31.   Flynn, A., Holmberg, S. R., Warren, D. T., & Wong, F. J. (2017). *The hidden rules of race: Barriers to an inclusive economy.* New York, NY: Cambridge University Press, p. 104. See also Irvine, J. J. (1991). *Black students and school failure.* New York, NY: Praeger; and Ladson-Billings, G. (2011). Boyz to men? Teaching to restore Black boys' childhood. *Race Ethnicity and Education, 14*(1), 7–15.

32.   This includes so-called good or positive stereotypes, which have been found to *negatively* influence teachers' perceptions of and interactions with some Asian American students. See, for example, Wallitt, R. (2008). Cambodian invisibility: Students lost between the "achievement gap" and the "model minority." *Multicultural Perspectives, 10*(1), 3–9; Zhao, Y., & Qiu, W. (2009). How good are the Asians? Refuting four myths about Asian-American academic achievement. *Phi Delta Kappan, 90*(5), 338–344.

33.   See, for example, Dovidio, J. (2001). On the nature of contemporary prejudice: The third wave. *Journal of Social Issues, 57*(4), 829–849; and Moule, J. (2009). Understanding unconscious bias and unintentional racism. *Phi Delta Kappan, 90*(5), 320–326.

34.   The Early Childhood Longitudinal Study Kindergarten (ECLS-K; 1999) followed students from kindergarten through eighth grade. This large data set began as a representative sample of over 20,000 students who entered kindergarten in 1999. By eighth grade, attrition (due to issues such as student movement, absence, and non-compliance) reduced the sample size. Our own sub-sample included 3,000 students who attended schools that offered algebra, but not to all students.

35.   The statistical results here were B = -.93; OR = .39; p < .0001. A one-unit change in this analysis is a standard deviation change of 1 because our variables have been transformed into z-scores. See Faulkner, V. N., Stiff, L. V., Marshall, P. L., Nietfeld, J., & Crossland, C. L. (2014). Race and teacher evaluations as predictors of algebra placement. *Journal for Research in Mathematics Education, 45*(3), 288–311.

36.   Also known as "mixed-ability" grouping, we will use the term heterogeneous here because it describes the idea that any group of humans are not uniform and are, indeed, a mix. On the other hand, mixed ability implies that someone has discerned students' abilities and then mixed them altogether. We argue that ability is somewhat unknowable and should not be a priority in instruction. Drawing on Dweck's (2006) research, we believe that teacher focus is more appropriately centered on the malleable demonstrations of *academic competencies* and not on finding ability levels. Competencies are verbs that can grow. Ability is a noun that is understood to be fixed.

37.   See, for example, Blackwell, Trzesniewski, & Dweck, 2007; Claro, Paunesku, & Dweck, 2016; Mouratidis, Michou, & Vassiou, 2017; and Romero, Master, Paunesku, Dweck, & Gross, 2014. See the following notes for full references.

38.   Blackwell, L. S., Trzesniewski, K. H., & Dweck, C. S. (2007). Implicit theories of intelligence predict achievement across an adolescent transition: A longitudinal study and an intervention. *Child Development, 78*(1), 246–263; and Claro, S., Paunesku, D., & Dweck, C. S. (2016). Growth mindset tempers the effects of poverty on academic achievement. *Proceedings of the National Academy of Sciences, 113*(31), 8664–8668.

39.   Mouratidis, A., Michou, A., & Vassiou, A. (2017). Adolescents' autonomous functioning and implicit theories of ability as predictors of their school achievement and week-to-week study regulation and well-being. *Contemporary Educational Psychology, 48*, 56–66.

40.   Romero, C., Master, A., Paunesku, D., Dweck, C. S., & Gross, J. J. (2014). Academic and emotional functioning in middle school: The role of implicit theories. *Emotion, 14*(2), 227.

41.   Different U.S. states designate these programs differently. Among the more common designations are "gifted," "gifted and talented," "academically gifted," and "talent identification." Irrespective of designation, all of these types of programs are based on the idea that young children can be identified as having *exceptional* intellectual gifts or talents.

42. Johnson, J., & Stiff, L. (2009). Who takes honors and advanced placement math? EDSTAR Analytics, Inc.

Chapter Four

Follow the Data

Gifts, Access, Cuts, and the Gap

In part I, we explored the tendency of professionals to use data doppels, such as socioeconomic status, race, gender, and other erroneous indicators, to make decisions. We also discussed the problematic nature of early identification of talent. Then, in chapter 3, we began our look at academic opportunities within schools by considering the complexities of classrooms in the United States.

Here, we continue our look at academic opportunity within schools and turn to school placement decision data. Using several sources, we will *follow the data* and listen to what it tells us about education professionals and the opportunities they provide or deny students.

Building on the discussion in chapter 3, we begin this chapter by considering the ideological constructs of providing a consistent curriculum for all students versus separating students into differentiated tiers of perceived ability or need. Based on how differential opportunity begins in elementary school, we consider gifted education. Identification for this top tier of placement opportunity tends to happen early—at about seven years of age. We will explore how the use of data is complicated by human intention. Indeed, here we will see how the use of data goes beyond efforts to weed out data doppels and into the mechanics of leveraging advantage for students. Finally, we follow the data by going beyond the use of test averages for groups and into examining actual data points.

RIGOR FOR ALL

One camp in educational theory holds that students should be taught within the same setting and held to the same high educational standards.[1] This viewpoint is in line with the idea that a "rising tide lifts all boats." In other words, ensuring access to the same rigorous content for all students will, on the whole, make for a stronger community of learners. This idea of providing rigor for all also removes the concern that academic ups and downs could affect a student's school placement and access to high standards and rigorous curriculum.

This approach to general education is consistent with the idea that a large part of intellectual progress comes from effort. In this scenario, all students, regardless of their background and potentially complex needs, are deemed worthy of access to a rigorous general curriculum, which can then be mastered with instructional support and effort. The idea of stratifying students into different intellectual levels is anathema to this rigor-for-all philosophy of education. To the contrary, intellectual success is seen as the goal for all students through access to the same rigorous curriculum over time.

The rigor-for-all camp is present within the current educational landscape. Rigor-for-all can be seen in schools where a conscious effort has been made to group students heterogeneously, rather than organizing students into tiered stratifications.[2] This approach is reinforced by researchers and mathematics educators who demonstrate methods for providing low-floor/high-ceiling instructional tasks that are accessible to all.[3] The rigor-for-all approach is consistent with ideas about how effort, rather than an innate gift, is more critical to learning. For instance, Carol Dweck's mindset work, along with research on expert performance, encourages the idea that intellectual capacity and educational attainment are not a fixed trait to be identified but a flexible capacity affected by effort, high expectations, opportunity, and rigorous instruction.

The rigor-for-all viewpoint is not new. In fact, a rising tide philosophy was evident in the first report of the National Education Association (NEA). In 1893 the NEA proposed that,

> Every subject which is taught at all in a secondary school should be taught in the same way and to the same extent to every pupil so long as he pursues it, no matter what the probable destination of the pupil may be or at what point his education is to cease.[4]

DIFFERENT STROKES

In the NEA's second report, the goal of education and the rhetoric used to describe it, had changed. In 1918[5] the spoken goals shifted. The idea behind the shift was that children would be better prepared for adulthood if their education met their future needs. This included restricting student course-taking opportunity by assigning students to different professional or vocational tracks. It was thereby argued that students are best prepared for a "democratic" society if their schooling matched their perceived potential contributions. We will, charitably, call this a "different strokes for different folks" approach.

The most extreme form of differentiation is providing different course-work in separate classrooms for students based on perceived needs. Another form of differentiation is putting students into perceived ability groups at the classroom level. Less extreme forms of differentiation[6] include providing different instructional supports within the same classroom space.

In the twenty-first century, differentiation that implies different curriculum for different students "has gradually dominated the debate, and it remains popular today."[7] Indeed, the rationale behind this 1918 change is uncannily current. Consider this summary, by Stevenson and Stigler, of the thinking present in 1918: "The old academic curriculum was virtually replaced by the so-called life-adjustment curriculum: An array of courses created to meet what educators perceived to be the range of needs and abilities in a diverse and rapidly increasing population."[8] In other words, this approach suggests that, given the complex nature of the world and the future roles students will have within that world, the burden of schools must shift from educating all students to identifying student capacity so as to match that capacity with a projected trajectory. If we accept that a primary role of education is to match student capacities to future life outcomes, then we must accept the need to anticipate what students can do *ahead of time*. Accepting this premise justifies differentially preparing students based on their *perceived potentials* or *perceived limited capacities*.

While many educators may believe that efforts to match potentials to outcomes is appropriate as students move through high school, the reality is that efforts to separate students into tiered levels of opportunity happens very early within the school experience. In the current landscape, a common way that educators provide different curricular experiences for different students is through gifted education.

A BRIEF HISTORY OF GIFTEDNESS

The idea that different humans have different capacities is not a new one, but quantifying those capacities with measurement tools and statistics is relatively new and reaches back only about a century. The early 1900s were a busy time for those aiming to demonstrate that human intelligence was measurable and that ranking humans by intelligence was, in different arenas, meaningful.

These early attempts to measure some meaningful construct of intelligence also included the implication that the information would be actionable. In other words, once the information was gathered, it could be used to make decisions, such as gaining entrance into the armed services.

While psychometricians, such as Galton, Stanford, and Binet, created this construct of intelligence, great ethical and moral questions were launched. These included questions about the legitimacy of these psychometrics to argue for or against the intelligence of an entire race and about the eventual use of eugenics to glean and shape populations.[9] We will not explore that history here, but do note that our discussion is tightly connected to the questions raised at that time. We are asking, in our own way, what does it mean to rank, rate, measure, and evaluate human capacity and what happens when we do? In this discussion of providing gifted status to some children, we engage with the ancestor of that earlier movement—the idea that intelligence is measurable, meaningful, and actionable. Once this idea is accepted, it easily becomes part of the complex dialogue regarding instructional decision-making and student placement in schools.

Currently, a crowning achievement for very young students in our public schools is being identified as "academically gifted." Sometimes called "gifted and talented" or just "gifted," this identification is like being picked for the elite academic team. Oftentimes, it entails being taught in a separate classroom for a period of time each week in elementary school and extends into greater opportunity for certain classes moving forward into secondary school.

Once identified as exceptional, these students are afforded opportunity to engage in more complex and rigorous academic curricula than their peers. Moreover, these students generally maintain this identification and the privileges it provides throughout their schooling years. This is because gifted status, once attained, often does not include any periodic reassessments.

While there are many ways to implement gifted education, a common elementary school model is to have students removed ("pulled out") from their current class at different times throughout the day or week to meet, along with fellow students also identified as gifted, with a teacher who specializes in the education of gifted students. Other elementary schools have moved to "pushing in" wherein the gifted educator provides curricular support and instructional ideas to the classroom teacher and for the benefit of the entire class. In both cases specific elementary school students are identified as gifted in order to receive special curricular considerations, teacher attention, and advanced coursework.

Access to the Gift

As academically gifted status grew from a small to a large percentage of students in the United States, [10] something became apparent: access to gifted status was racially and socioeconomically skewed. Recently, this phenomenon has been studied more intensively, and these racialized trends have remained consistent to this day. [11] At the same time, access to gifted status has long-term consequences for student opportunity. For this reason, it is widely and compellingly argued that gifted education is "the first important stage of racialized tracking in the nation's public schools." [12]

This argument has reached the proponents of the gifted education movement. James Borland, of Columbia Teachers College in New York City, and a leader in the field of gifted education, edited and contributed to the book *Rethinking Gifted Education.* [13] In his introduction, Borland acknowledges and validates the consistent critiques of gifted education regarding inequitable access to opportunity and services. He sees the need to end defensive reactions designed to protect the ideas and institutions of gifted education and to, instead, look openly at the criticisms and the data. Because he believes that the charges of inequity "were serious charges . . . backed by hard data," he validates that "defending gifted programs missed the point." [14]

Borland addresses two points pertinent to this discussion. [15] First, he questions the very nature of identifying some students as gifted. He argues that, indeed, depending on one's school district and the specifics of identification, children are deemed gifted in one place and nongifted in another. Borland calls this "geographical giftedness." This geographical giftedness is an acknowledgment that decisions about who is gifted require social constructs and professional judgments. Notably, the systems put in place to identify students are failing to identify students equitably. As Borland summarizes the research on this point, he states that "Racial inequalities in the identification of gifted students have been a constant throughout [gifted education] history." [16] The second point Borland makes concerns pull-out programming. Borland identifies this practice as problematic because, in effect, pull-out gifted programming serves to segregate students by socioeconomic status and race. [17]

The Cut

So how does gifted programming serve to segregate students within a school district and what can the data tell us? David Card and Laura Giuliano, writing for the National Bureau of Economic Research, analyzed a naturally occurring data set [18] to understand patterns and practice for identifying students as gifted. The district they studied was one of the "largest and most diverse" school districts in the United States. [19]

As is common practice in school districts across the country, this district identified second graders (seven to eight years old) to assess for gifted status based on teacher referral. The professional judgment of the teacher, therefore, played a large part in the screening process. Parent referral was also used, which is also a common practice. With this referral-based screening system in place, Black and Hispanic students, who represented 60% of the district population, represented 28% of the students identified for gifted education. Put another way, the 40% of White and Asian American students were "drafted" into 72% of the gifted spots.[20]

In this district, under the status quo system, the professional recommendations of educators (and requests from parents) served as a screening process that greatly lessened the pool of students who went on to take the tests required for placement in the gifted program. As with female musicians before blinded auditions, the screening mechanism of *who gets invited to apply* greatly reduces the pool of candidates and does so in favor of some over others. While the assessments are uniform, *choosing who gets to take the assessment* is not.

This same school system then changed its protocol away from the referral system and provided funding to perform universal screening to generate the candidate pool to be assessed for gifted status. This eliminated the referral cut and, instead, allowed all students to actively engage in the quest to be a part of the school's elite pool of talent.[21] This protocol began in 2005. Black student placement in academically gifted programming went up 80%, and placement of Hispanic students went up 130%.[22]

Not only did more students get identified for gifted education without a change in the required minimum entry score, but the "newly discovered" gifted students were disproportionately poor, Black, and Hispanic.[23] Critically, they found that "the distribution of IQ scores for the newly identified students was very similar to the distribution among those who were identified under the referral system."[24] Moreover, this included "many students with IQ's *significantly above the minimum eligibility threshold*" [emphasis added].[25] As with our own findings, this implies that even students with *very high performance* are blocked from opportunity when a traditional, referral-based protocol is employed. Not unlike the emergency department described in chapter 2, a change to a standardized protocol removed distractors and improved the professionals' ability to identify those students qualified to access services.

Not surprisingly, the students of color and poorer students who were identified during the universal screening years benefited from their gifted status. Their achievement gains in third and fourth grades were evident and at least as strong as the students who likely would have been identified without universal screening. These students, who would have been overlooked under the status quo referral system, were indeed up to the challenge and performed well when provided the opportunity they earned.[26]

Before this universal screening system was put in place, high-performing and capable students of color were consistently unacknowledged and denied access to the opportunities for which they were qualified. This inequity was largely resolved merely by substituting referral-based barriers with performance data and universal access to opportunity.

On a path to equitable access, this system now had evidence that its pool of talent was large and diverse. Students who were perceived unworthy of making the cut by referral were now attaining gifted status.

Unfortunately, rather than continuing down that path, the system disbanded the new protocols that bolstered student access. Citing the great recession of 2008, the universal screening protocol was revoked in 2010.

Faced with returning to a professional protocol that demonstrated systematic oversights in referral, one might expect a different outcome the next time around. Perhaps lessons learned during the universal screening years would prompt educators to look harder for referrals from previously underrepresented groups. And perhaps some did. But the data does not support the idea that these professionals, again required to rely on the traditional referral-based protocol, subsequently changed their habits of practice.

By the next school year, the earlier placement patterns reemerged in the district with previous levels of disproportionate placement of White and Asian American students. Accordingly, Card and Giuliano conclude that a substantial share of the gap in placement into gifted programs "appears to be caused by the failure of the traditional parent/teacher referral system to identify high-ability disadvantaged students."[27]

FOLLOWING DATA

This failure is noteworthy. The demographic oversights exposed during the universal screening years and the discovery of a new pool of talent were not enough to change habits of mind and patterns of practice. Again, consider that the educators in this school district *had the data* indicating that the practice of using a referral-based protocol *contributed to a consistent loss of qualified students*. If the stated goal is to identify students performing at high levels and the local data has made it clear that the referral system does not do that, wouldn't a reasonable response be to put some low-cost safeguard in place to make sure all qualified students are discovered? Even with the loss of funds, is there not some professional responsibility to continue to locate these high achievers?

We argue that there is such a professional responsibility to address the inequitable outcomes of a status quo referral system, but the data suggest that was not the lesson learned. Instead, *when it came to acknowledging the academic ability of Black and Hispanic students,* old habits die hard. The reemergence of inequitable patterns found in the data tells us that, for this community of professionals, the habits didn't die at all.

The issue of unequal access to gifted services is not unique to this one study or this one community. To the contrary, these findings and the reactions to these types of findings are the norm. For instance, investigative journalists explored student data for all school districts in North Carolina, and similar patterns emerged regarding access to gifted programming.[28] In this study the focus of analysis was not on race but socioeconomic status. The analysis of statewide data showed that students of lower-income levels were also consistently underrepresented in gifted classes. In fact, the reporters found that "In several large school systems, more nonpoor students who test at grade level are labeled gifted than are low-income students who score above grade level, or superior."[29] In other words, socioeconomic status, clearly a data doppel with regard to academic performance, overrides pertinent academic data for a large number of students.

Campbell's Law

Before leaving the issue of gaining gifted status, let's consider this topic from a slightly different angle. Specifically, what does it mean to decide that a certain measure captures the quality of giftedness and what happens once that decision is made in a community?

Turning characteristics of human spirit and performance into a quantitative value has a certain appeal in that it allows us to make sense of our world and the people in it. At the same time, measuring and evaluating people within a system is not a simple proposition. Not only do we need to consider questions of construct validity (what are we actually measuring and does it matter?), but we also need to understand the impact of the measurement itself.

Measuring a decided-upon characteristic can have an impact on the value of measuring that characteristic. Once what is being measured becomes known, the measurement itself takes on a new life. In an effort to gain advantage, behaviors are molded by the knowledge of the measurement. Known as Campbell's law to social scientists and systems evaluators, it suggests that "When a measure becomes a target, it ceases to be a good measure."[30] We believe that educators and parents and other community members must consider the phenomenon of Campbell's law, which speaks to the very use of data itself. Richard Hess, who has written extensively on this topic,[31] puts it this way:

When you put a lot of weight on a given measure, people react. When they do, it can mess up the measure while creating incentives you never anticipated. What at first seems like a smart, clever, and cutting-edge way to use data can look very different in hindsight. [32]

Does Campbell's law affect our lives or is it purely an academic idea? Consider these examples put forth by Hess and summarized here. The first involves flight times in the United States and, the second, factories in the former Soviet Union.

One might think that evaluating airlines based on their ability to transport people in the time frame they advertise would be a good thing and would create an incentive to improve overall flight times. Think again. Measuring on-time flights and evaluating airlines in relation to on-time data *increased average flight times.* Why? Because airlines adjusted policies in an effort to generate high marks for on-time status. They began to post less ambitious arrival times so that they could be considered on time without improving performance. Now, customers board earlier and sit on the tarmac longer. From 1989, when the policy of using on-time data was put in place, through 1999, flights from New York to Seattle took an average of 22 minutes and 48 seconds longer. [33] So measuring on-time status served to increase flight times.

Now, consider Soviet factories. Rather than being evaluated on "softer" performance variables, such as customer satisfaction or product quality, factory supervisors were evaluated based on discrete performance indicators that could be measured. So what happened? When quotas were set based on tonnage of output, products simply got heavier. Similarly, when quotas were based on number of products produced, odd things also happened. For instance, cars came off the assembly line missing key components, like an engine.

How might this relate to identifying students as academically gifted? Consider an IQ test score used to identify gifted students. These are initially performed within the school setting. But, with a clear target available, individual families of means are able to leverage their resources toward gaining access to gifted education for their child.

Some families, for example, pay for their children to receive tutoring aimed specifically at improving scores on intelligence tests. Others have their children tested by private evaluators and present the resulting test scores to the schools. Private psychological testing is costly, generally around $1,000 per child, and is not a viable option for most families. [34] But, once presented to them, public school personnel are obligated to accept these scores and act accordingly by granting gifted status.

Gaming the system in this way is an understood reality within schools. There are students who gain access to gifted education through concerted, and often quite costly, efforts to achieve the target score. Evidence for this includes a spike in test scores around the gifted qualification mark connected to students with higher socioeconomic status.[35] So a data point ostensibly used to objectively identify students for gifted status instead identifies students from families with the socioeconomic means to "game" that data point.[36]

BEYOND GIFTED

Schools are grounded on a rich and complex soil of ideas and initiatives. Once an idea is planted (such as the idea to provide differentiated educational experiences), it can take root quickly and grow beyond expectation. We have connected the idea of differentiated school experiences to that of measuring intelligence and identifying students as academically gifted. And we have considered the problematic nature of using a referral protocol or a game-able data point to identify students as gifted. But the urge to stratify lives on.

Another mechanism for stratifying young students is "single subject acceleration." In this model, elementary-aged students are placed in mathematics classes that are above their current grade level. A second grader, for instance, could be identified to work in the third grade math curriculum with other identified second graders or within a third grade class itself. Such a model requires school personnel to identify students qualified for this specific curricular leap.

A 2017 investigative piece examined the patterns and practices of single subject acceleration programs.[37] In particular, investigators studied a large urban school district in the Southeast that adopted this practice a few years prior to the report. While the policy in this district calls for a "consistent, fair, and systematic" approach to providing the opportunity to all students, outcomes do not reflect that goal. Of the students identified for advancement, 90% were White or Asian American.[38] This was the outcome in a school district with 55% White or Asian American students. From a different angle, the Black and Hispanic students, who make up 40% of the students in the district, represented only 5%, or 1 out of every 20 students, identified for the single subject acceleration program. In raw numbers, that is 32 identified Black and Hispanic students out of over 600 students identified for the program.

The Referral Pool

In response to the data regarding the single subject acceleration program in this district, the school system's chief officer for data and accountability is reported to have offered no clear answers for the discrepancies. Lacking clear answers, the officer, quite appropriately, speculated about the referral pool and indicated that the district has "groups that we struggle to get information to." This implies that the lack of referrals could be because the parents weren't aware of the opportunity. So, here, a reasonable concern follows from this data. A reasonable response would be to address the problems with the referral pool.

If a capable population is systematically underrepresented throughout an identification process, check to see how one gains entry into the applicant pool. Following that logic, a solution might be to add universal screening to ensure that all students have the opportunity to score well on the assessment that confers access to the program. Or perhaps, rather than an informal referral system, academic data could be used for screening purposes. In the 2017 article reported above, no solution along these lines was proffered.

GAP-LOGIC

The school chief officer described above in the 2017 article also said this, "When you use prior achievement as your criteria, any kind of achievement gap there might be is going to be reflected."[39] Here, prior academic achievement data is being positioned as a barrier and as something that *hurts* the chances of Black and Hispanic students gaining admission into the program. We call this "gap-logic."

Here is how gap-logic works. The landscape of student performance is defined by the gap. Therefore, using academic data to determine individual admission to a program will likewise mirror the gap. Essentially, gap-logic implies that educators' placement decisions about individual students are *hamstrung by the poor group performance of Black and Hispanic students.*

The Achievement-Gap Mean

Clearly, a critical part of gap-logic is the construct of a demographically organized achievement gap. Gap-logic uses the group's mean[40] of student academic performance on a particular indicator to quantify individual student experience and to demonstrate the existence of a gap. For instance, you can see in figure 4.1 a fairly typical depiction. Here, we have data displayed using the mean scores of Black and White students in Maryland on recent rounds of the National Assessment of Educational Progress. This is the classic depiction of what has been consistently called an achievement gap. The average performance of White students for this large data set is consistently higher than the average performance of Black students in the same state and taking the same assessments.

In the case of academic performance, a mean provides one number to describe many students. Often, *one mean* describes an entire nation of students or an entire state, region, or township. Quite commonly, we organize

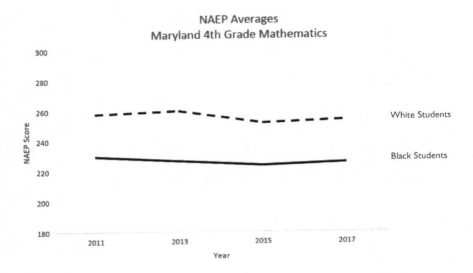

Figure 4.1. The Gap as a Mean: Maryland National Association of Educational Progress Math Scores. *Source*: Adapted from http://www.maryland publicschools.org/stateboard/Documents/05222018/TabJ-NAEPResults.pdf

student data by demographic background, and the mean provides one number to describe a vast array of students.

The mean does not speak to individual student understandings, experiences, needs, or achievements. Likewise, the mean does not translate into any significantly useful assessment of individual performance or instructional need.

If one has an understanding of individual students that relies on this demonstration of compared means (particularly if achievement characteristics are perceived as immutable and naturally occurring), then there is a logic that using prior achievement data will not help identify high-performing Black students. But such logic is flawed. Students do not perform in lockstep with the demographic categories placed upon them, nor do they perform in lockstep with the averages used to represent them.

VARIANCE AND VARIETY

When we examine student academic achievement, we see a great deal of variety in student performance. People and students of different backgrounds perform in different ways. This is both logical, and we imagine, something most of us see in our everyday experiences.

Using a small set of constructed data to illustrate, let's look at the idea of variety. Let's imagine a situation where there are 20 students. In keeping with the percentages described just above, let's also allow 55% of our students to be classified as White and 45% Black or Hispanic. In raw numbers that will be 11 and 9 students, respectively.

In our data set, we suppose an overall average of 75.5%. Looking at demographic data we suppose average scores of 80% (White students) and 70% (Black/Hispanic students), so there is a fairly large gap in performance. But the reality of a set of group data is that there are ups and downs of individual student performance. In other words, there is variance in the data. In figure 4.2 we see our class of students not through the lens of group demographics but through the lens of individual performance. We have organized students by a performance indicator. So what do you see? You see students who performed well on an assessment and students who performed not as well on an assessment.

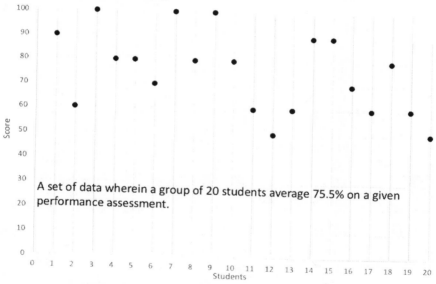

A set of data wherein a group of 20 students average 75.5% on a given performance assessment.

Figure 4.2. A sample set of performance data for a class of 20

This display then begs the question, If this is your understanding of student achievement, where might you look for high performers? For instance, How would you find the students who scored 80% or above on this measure? As seen in figure 4.3, this is a fairly simple matter. You would need to identify those students performing above a criterion. In this case, there are 11 students who demonstrated a scored performance of 80% or above. This display of the data demonstrates how individual academic performance must be analyzed and understood at an individual academic performance level.

Chapter 4

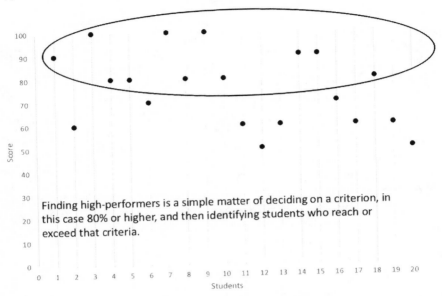

Finding high-performers is a simple matter of deciding on a criterion, in this case 80% or higher, and then identifying students who reach or exceed that criteria.

Figure 4.3.   Finding high performers in our class set of 20

Now, notice that in figure 4.4 we have uncovered the demographic data. This cutoff at 80 yields a set of identified students with seven White students and four students of color. White students, who represent 55% of the population, are slightly overrepresented (7 out of 11 is 64%). Likewise, students of color (45% of the population) are slightly underrepresented (4 out of 11 is 36%). Nevertheless, this scenario demonstrates how, even with a group gap in achievement, individual students from different demographic groups are worthy of placement. *The gap in average performance does not determine individual merit and does not logically indicate that accelerated programs would be grossly overrepresented by one demographic group.*

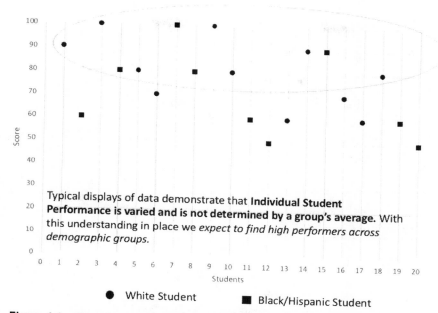

Typical displays of data demonstrate that **Individual Student Performance is varied and is not determined by a group's average.** With this understanding in place we *expect to find high performers across demographic groups.*

Figure 4.4. **Free the data: Revealing demographics without considering the mean**

The Mean Doesn't Mean What You Think It Means

In the above examples, we saw how the mean was not useful for identifying individual high performance. In figure 4.5, we reveal the means for this set of students and again see how the mean does not provide any information about where to look for high performers. The mean is not meant to identify individual high performance; indeed, it is designed to do just the opposite! The mean is designed to look at group trends. Just as an inequitable system in hockey was uncovered by looking at the trend of birthdates, so might we identify inequitable trends in education by looking at means.

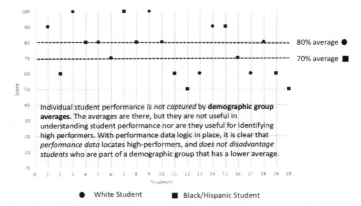

The chart contains the text:

Individual student performance *is not captured* by **demographic group averages.** The averages are there, but they are not useful in understanding student performance nor are they useful for identifying high performers. With performance data logic in place, it is clear that *performance data* locates high-performers, and *does not disadvantage students* who are part of a demographic group that has a lower average.

● White Student   ■ Black/Hispanic Student

Figure 4.5. Revealing the mean does not inform decisions about finding high-performing students

So why would the idea of an achievement gap even enter into a conversation about identifying individual high achievers? Perhaps it is habit to assume that one group of students doesn't perform as well as another group; therefore, "the gap" becomes a cultural shortcut. This shortcut then serves to justify why opportunities are provided to some students and not others.

FINDING STUDENTS

For better or worse,[41] school personnel seek to provide higher levels of academic access for some students. Earlier, we described how universal screening using academic data will most likely *increase* the number of Black and Hispanic students identified for these opportunities.[42] At the same time, we have seen how the mean provides no information about the exceptionally high-performing individuals in a population.

By invoking gap-logic, one implies that the statistical tool of an *average* is pertinent in an active search to identify *nonaverage* students. Gap-logic is revealed when one conceives, consciously or unconsciously, that people perform academically in a way that can be predicted by their demographic category.

With a gap-logic conception of the data, one assumes that the mean speaks to an entire group of students' academic needs. With this conception of the data, *and without universal screening to keep that conception in check*, inequitable patterns of placement will indeed "snap back into place" as we saw above with regard to referrals for gifted programming. This conception of the group data justifies and permits widely disproportionate placements of one group of students over another. This conception of the data also supports the logic that using academic data would *hurt* Black and Hispanic students.

On the other hand, if one conceives of and internalizes the reality of student performance as containing variance, then gap-logic rationale is exposed as ill-conceived. What's more, the understanding that student performance is quite variable reveals a solution to finding high performers. That solution is that educators must ditch the data doppel of demographic means and "see" the academic performance of individual students.

In our next section, we consider the specifics of decision-making in schools. In chapter 5, we use case studies from schools to understand how the issue of access to high-level, rigorous mathematics coursework plays out for specific students. We will explore what happened when a school decided to follow the data, remove data doppels, and place students in a pre-algebra class based on a systematic review of academic criteria.

NOTES

1. For this discussion of educational history, we draw from Stevenson and Stigler's reporting of Richard Hofstadter (1963) and his analysis of the primary documents from the National Education Association. Stevenson, H., & Stigler, J. (1992). *The learning gap: Why our schools are failing and what we can learn from Japanese and Chinese education.* New York, NY: Simon & Schuster, Chapter 5, Effort and Ability.

2. Darity, W. A., & Jolla, A. (2009). Desegregated schools with segregated education. In C. Hartman & G. Squires (Eds.), *The integration debate: Competing futures for American cities* (pp. 99–117). New York, NY: Routledge.

3. See, for instance, Boaler, J. (2015). *Mathematical mindsets: Unleashing students' potential through creative math, inspiring messages and innovative teaching.* San Francisco, CA: Jossey-Bass.

4. This quote comes from the NEA report, *Anti-Intellectualism in American Life,* as quoted in Richard Hofstadter (1963) and reported in Stevenson, H., & Stigler, J. (1992). *The learning gap: Why our schools are failing and what we can learn from Japanese and Chinese education.* New York, NY: Simon & Schuster, p. 107.

5. While beyond the scope of this discussion, it is interesting to think about contemporary events in 1918. Perhaps the mood of the NEA was related to recent engagement in a world war, the introduction of intelligence testing, the great influenza epidemic, and a reigniting of racial tensions after the movie *The Birth of a Nation.*

6. Differentiation is a word that has its own life in current educational practice. In the rising tide approach the word "differentiation" implies teaching all students the same curricular content together and to do so with low-floor/high-ceiling tasks. These tasks are designed to engage all students by providing different access points into the same conversation. At the same time, some people use the word "differentiation" to mean providing students different curricular experiences within the same classroom. For instance, teachers might differentiate in this context by providing some students different worksheets or homework. Or they may design separate lessons for small groups based on specific needs. These two approaches are not mutually exclusive. At the same time, the actualization of the philosophies depends on the greater context in which differentiation is interpreted, as described here.

7. Stevenson, H., & Stigler, J. (1992). *The learning gap: Why our schools are failing and what we can learn from Japanese and Chinese education.* New York, NY: Simon & Schuster, p. 107.

8. Stevenson, H., & Stigler, J. (1992). *The learning gap: Why our schools are failing and what we can learn from Japanese and Chinese education.* New York, NY: Simon & Schuster, p. 108.

9. We will not explore this period here, but it is a rich period for exploration. One book of particular interest on this topic is Gould, S. J. (1981). *The mismeasure of man*. New York, NY: W.W. Norton & Company.

10. Out of approximately 50 million children in U.S. public schools, more than 3 million (6%) are identified as academically gifted (from National Association of Gifted Children at http://www.nagc.org/resources-publications/resources/gifted-education-us). Reviewing state websites associated with the National Association of Gifted Children reveals that there is a wide range, school by school and state by state, in how this plays out. For instance, in North Carolina, 180,000 out of 1,400,000 students (13%) are identified as gifted; Nevada, 12,500 students out of 460,000 students (2.5%); Maine, 7,000 out of 183,000 (4%); and Indiana, 140,000 out of 1,000,000 (14%).

11. Darity, W. A., & Jolla, A. (2009). Desegregated schools with segregated education. In C. Hartman & G. Squires (Eds.), *The integration debate: Competing futures for American cities* (pp. 99–117). New York, NY: Routledge.

12. Ibid., p. 107.

13. Borland, J. H. (Ed.). (2003). *Rethinking gifted education*. New York, NY: Teachers College Press.

14. Borland, 2003, p. 2.

15. He also makes some points that contradict our own theses. In particular, Borland supports the idea of accelerated curriculum, which we discuss here in chapter 4. Likewise, he does not go so far as to suggest the elimination of gifted services in spite of the many conceptual and practical flaws he considers. Nevertheless, he clearly establishes the arguments we highlight here and his overall concern—inequities instantiated in gifted education—is compatible with our own.

16. Borland, 2003, p. 117.

17. Borland acknowledges, but does not countenance, the use of gifted programs to stem "white flight." He cites Sapon-Shevin, M. (1994). *Playing favorites: Gifted education and the disruption of community*. Albany, NY: SUNY Press, along with his own experience, to acknowledge this reality.

18. A naturally occurring data set is one that arises from a condition in the environment that the researcher did not create. In this instance, the funds available to institute universal screening changed the conditions in the schools. While a researcher did not manipulate or organize these conditions, the data generated before and after the changes occurred are nevertheless available to be studied.

19. Card, D., & Giuliano, L. (2015). *Can universal screening increase the representation of low income and minority students in gifted education?* (No. w21519). National Bureau of Economic Research, p. 1.

20. If that does not seem shocking to you, remind yourself how you would respond if we said that the 40% of players born early in the year received 72% of the draft picks in a sport.

21. To be clear, the new system used a universal screening tool to locate students not for admittance but to take the test required for entry into the gifted program. Students from populations that had been formerly overlooked via the *referral* system were held to a lower cutoff score on the screening tool to ensure all possible candidates were identified and placed into the next round toward admittance. All candidates who made the screening cut were provided the opportunity to take the assessment to gain entry into the gifted program. Once taken, only admittance-level scores on the gifted assessment were accepted, and no allowance was made in granting gifted status (Card & Giuliano, 2015).

22. These statistics do not mean that the numbers drew even, but these percentages do represent a substantial shift in access.

23. Other groups benefited from the universal screening as well. Students with lower socioeconomic background, students learning English as a second language, and girls benefited from the new protocol. This implies that these groups of students were also underidentified using the professional/parent referral system.

24. Card & Giuliano, 2015, p. 3.

25. Card & Giuliano, 2015, p. 3.

26. Card & Giuliano, 2015.

27. Card & Giuliano, 2015, p. 23.

28. Long, T., Neff, J., Helms, A. D., & Raynor, D. (2017, May 21). Why have thousands of smart, low-income NC students been excluded from advanced classes? *The News & Observer.* Retrieved from http://www.newsobserver.com/news/local/education/article149942987.html.

29. As an example, Long et al. cited these statistics from a large and representative district: "228 low-income third-graders scored a 5—superior, or above grade level—on their math end-of-grade tests and did not get into a gifted math class the following year. Yet 291 more affluent students who scored a 4—solid, or at grade level—qualified as gifted." Long, T., Neff, J., Helms, A. D., & Raynor, D. (2017, May 21). Why have thousands of smart, low-income NC students been excluded from advanced classes? *The News & Observer.* Retrieved from http://www.newsobserver.com/news/local/education/article149942987.html.

30. Hess, R. (2018, June 12). Education reforms should obey Campbell's law. *Education Week.* Retrieved from http://blogs.edweek.org/edweek/rick_hess_straight_up/2018/06/education_reforms_should_obey_campbells_law.html.

31. Hess, F. M. (2017). *Letters to a young education reformer.* Cambridge, MA: Harvard Education Press; and Hess, R. (2018, June 12). Education reforms should obey Campbell's law. *Education Week.* Retrieved from http://blogs.edweek.org/edweek/rick_hess_straight_up/2018/06/education_reforms_should_obey_campbells_law.html.

32. Hess, R. (2018, June 12). Education reforms should obey Campbell's law. *Education Week.* Retrieved from http://blogs.edweek.org/edweek/rick_hess_straight_up/2018/06/education_reforms_should_obey_campbells_law.html.

33. These examples are from Hess (2018).

34. Note that the independent psychologist has an array of assessments available to him or her, such as nonverbal measures. Children sometimes take several assessments until they get a "hit" that qualifies them for gifted status.

35. Card, D., & Giuliano, L. (2014). *Does gifted education work? For which students?* (No. w20453). National Bureau of Economic Research.

36. This phenomenon of Campbell's law applies to the evaluation of teachers as well. This was hinted at in chapter 3 as the accountability culture pervades schools. Consider this quote from Hess: "In education, improvement efforts have frequently been blindsided by Campbell's law. Attempts to evaluate schools and teachers using a few simple metrics, primarily reading and math scores, have given educators cause to do everything possible to boost those results—to the point that it has sometimes brought to mind those old Soviet factories" (Hess, 2018).

37. Goldsmith, T. (2017, May 24). A Wake schools program helps white, Asian, and male students advance in math. Black, Hispanic, and female students? Not so much. *Indyweek.* Retrieved from https://indyweek.com/news/wake-schools-program-helps-white-asian-male-students-advance-math.-black-hispanic-female-students-much./.

38. Again, as with the Card and Giuliani study on gifted identification reported above, girls were also underidentified. There were twice as many boys identified for the program as girls.

39. We use this example not because it is unique or unexpected but because the logic it holds is pervasive in our school culture. We therefore suggest educators should worry less about fault or blame and more about understanding arguments using, or failing to use, data to describe, or locate, highly achieving students.

40. Many people say average when what they actually are referring to is the mean. In mathematical parlance, there are many ways to make sense of data and consider what is average. One way to consider the data is through totaling up a value for all the data points and dividing by the number of data points to get one number to represent the data set. That is a *mean.* Another way is to think about what is the *most common* thing that happened in the data set. That is known as the *mode.* A third way is to consider what the middle point is in the data set. That is called the *median.* Then, a fourth way, which is sort of wild and crazy, is to break the data into quartiles and see how the data spreads out. That is commonly called a box and whisker plot. Here, we will use the word "mean" to indicate the mean, what some might think of in common parlance as "average."

41. Recall that we are not arguing for stratifications such as these, but, if they exist, we are arguing for equitable placement into the programs.

42. We will have another example of this in chapter 6.

III

Decision-Making in Schools

Chapter Five

When Teachers Push Back

Data versus Belief

Throughout this book, we have considered how opportunity and access to rigorous academics is affected by many systems and habits of practice that are enacted within the professional community of schools. When it comes to schools, these systems and habits range from early identification of perceived ability to the use of nonacademic data to justify academic placement decisions. We have considered large data sets that demonstrate a denial of academic opportunity for students of color and students of lower socioeconomic status even when they demonstrate strong performance. The data does not seem to drive the decisions. And, as we have seen, access to rigorous mathematics and advanced opportunity is skewed in favor of some students over others.

To understand what it looks like when capable students are actively prevented from gaining access to rigorous mathematics opportunities or are simply ignored, we will now consider specific decisions and responses that involve data within classrooms and schools. With this, we will show how individual acts of decision-making and professional judgment contribute to the systemic patterns we have explored. To that end, we revisit actual cases in which students, in spite of objective data, were denied access to high-quality mathematics instruction and accelerated content.[1] This will reveal what it looks like when educators push back against data and the documented performance of students.

MATHEMATICS COURSE PLACEMENT

As educators decide what mathematics instruction is appropriate for a given set of students, it seems reasonable to assert that students should be evaluated to determine the types of experiences they need to be successful in mathematics. Often, student strengths and needs can be met without a variety of high and low mathematical course offerings. With appropriate tasks and the right approach, students can work through the same mathematical content objectives with students who have different specific strengths and needs. This is, indeed, how many countries with high-performance math results do business. [2]

At the same time, most school districts in the United States decide to differentiate mathematics opportunities for students through different course offerings or academic experiences. These experiences happen throughout elementary school within the classroom and through special services, such as those for students identified as academically gifted. By middle school, these different academic experiences are generally solidified into different courses with different levels.

THE PLACEMENT DECISION

It seems obvious that, if these academic levels are put into place, then students' course-taking opportunities should be based on objective achievement criteria tied to individual student performance. This is self-evident in that the stated objective for creating different course or class levels is because of the academic strengths and needs of the student.

Unfortunately, while the use of academic criteria is a simple and effective solution for identifying students performing at a high level at a given time, what constitutes the academic data becomes complicated by habit, practice, culture, and judgment. Even so, there is often a stated goal, within a school or district, that placement decisions and instructional intervention decisions should rely more heavily on objective performance data and less on teachers' or counselors' perceptions of students.

PROFESSIONAL BELIEFS

To be sure, in our work with educators, we find that teachers and administrators initially agree to the use of objective achievement criteria as a means to determine placement in mathematics classes. The planned use of data, from what we have seen, is consistent with background belief stories the educators may hold about their role as decision-makers.

This initial agreement may align with the professional belief regarding their own ability to perceive student academic performance level. In other words, educators may believe that the students who will gain access to high-quality math courses will be the same students they would have otherwise selected using their own professional judgment. Regardless of the exact mechanics, in our experience, educators endorse the idea of using objective performance data to make decisions about students. Perhaps initial lists are made and the names of students are lined up on paper for course placement opportunities based on performance. But, then, something else happens.[3]

ADJUSTMENTS: CHANGING THE RULES OF ENGAGEMENT

A common pathway for students through their mathematics journey includes being separated by perceived ability. While this generally happens in elementary school via grouping practices within a classroom, it becomes formalized in middle school. For instance, it has become common for middle school students to be separated into two "tracks" in sixth and seventh grade depending on whether students are deemed to be prepared to begin pre-algebra work that will lead to taking Algebra 1 in eighth grade (see table 5.1). The placement decisions for this pathway are often based on teacher or parent referral.

Fifth Grade	Sixth Grade	Seventh Grade	Eighth Grade	High School Trajectory
5th Grade Math Standards	6th Grade Math Standards – Advanced Level	Pre-Algebra	Algebra/Math I	Geometry/Math II *Privileged Access to Highest Level Math Courses Associated with High Academic and Financial Outcomes*
	6th Grade Math Standards – Regular Level	7th Grade Math Standards	8th Grade Math Standards	Algebra/Math I
				Pre-Algebra

Table 5.1.   **Course-taking trajectories before district-wide policy put into place. Students placed in courses primarily based on teacher referral or parent request.**

In one urban Southeastern school district, a new school board policy was designed to standardize placement according to students' demonstrated mathematical performance. The criteria for placement into the top track of sixth grade mathematics were as follows:

> In addition to sharing work samples, students must satisfy two of three criteria: (a) have a supportive teacher recommendation, (b) score at a high Level IV or at Level V[4] on the End-of-Grade (EOG) assessment, and (c) receive a grade no lower than a 3 (out of 4) on their standards-based report cards.

The expectation was that, if students met two of the three objective achievement criteria, they would be recommended for the top track of middle school mathematics coursework.

Given the opportunity, virtually all students, and especially students of color, will outperform the low-performing labels that have been assigned to them.[5] Unfortunately, even when students embrace opportunities and excel, teachers' individual and collective reactions to the *successful* academic performance of students can be disappointing. As found in the example from chapter 2, where 103 sixth graders in a single school were "adjusted" out of the top track in mathematics, the rules of engagement can be fluid.

The Rules

As background for our first case, in the urban school district in the Southeast described previously, the school board passed a policy that stated all schools within the district must place middle-school students into courses according to academic criteria. In particular, placement into the highest course in sixth grade (the course that would lead to enrollment in algebra by eighth grade) required meeting specific academic targets (see policy outlined above). The goal was to ensure that all students have access to high-quality mathematics instruction based on their prior achievement (see table 5.2). The policy would go into effect the following school year.

Fifth Grade	RULE	Sixth Grade	Seventh Grade	Eighth Grade	High School Trajectory
	Inconsistent Leadership				
5th Grade Math Standards	School Board Policy	6th Grade Math Standards – Advanced Level	7th & 8th Grade Standards: Pre-Algebra	Algebra/Math I	Geometry/Math II *Standardized Access to Highest Level Math Courses Associated with High Academic and Financial Outcomes*
		6th Grade Math Standards – Regular Level	7th Grade Math Standards	8th Grade Math Standards	Algebra/Math I — Pre-Algebra

Table 5.2. **Course-taking trajectories after district-wide policy put into place to standardize placement policy. The policy criteria included high performance on standardized assessments, high course performance in math, and teacher recommendation. Students who met two of the three criteria were to be placed into advanced coursework leading to Algebra/Math I by the 8th grade. The Case of Inconsistent Leadership (described later in this chapter) is identified in these course trajectories.**

Just after the policy was passed, the school district created a new top track for students—Algebra I in the seventh grade. The school board policy designed to create equitable placements as students advanced toward Algebra I by the eighth grade did not include this new top-track option as part of its mandate. As a consequence, the "elite students" would again be offered opportunities different than those otherwise available to all students in the system, per the new board placement policy. Moreover, not all students and parents were made aware of the changes that would allow students to pursue the new top-track seventh grade Algebra I option.

To take algebra in the seventh grade, special "Compacted 6/7" math classrooms were created for sixth graders. In turn, a pipeline that would move students into the Compacted 6/7 math classrooms was created in the guise of Compacted 5/6 math classrooms in some, but not all, elementary schools (see table 5.3). As it turned out, elementary schools without full-time gifted education teachers were not able to provide a Compacted 5/6 math course for their students. This is because it was full-time gifted education teachers who were charged with providing these particular courses.

In the same year that the school board implemented the policy for all students to have fair and equitable access to eighth grade algebra, some elementary students were effectively blocked from access to the new opportunity to take algebra by seventh grade by virtue of their current elementary school placement. Furthermore, at the schools where the opportunity was available, for elementary students to get into the pipeline of opportunity, there was no checklist or systematic board policy in place to screen for or identify those students. And so, in the absence of a formal policy, some students were specially selected for placement in Compacted 5/6 math classes. These students would then feed the Compacted 6/7 math classrooms in the following year when the new course-taking trajectories would go into effect.

Fifth Grade	RULE	Sixth Grade	Seventh Grade	Eighth Grade	High School Trajectory
Alexander					
5th/6th Math * No Standardized Placement Rule * Not available at all schools	None	6 &7 Grade 'compacted' Math	Algebra/Math I	Geometry/Math II	Math III *Privileged Access to Highest Level Math Courses and Associated Outcomes*
				Laila	
5th Grade Math Standards	School Board Policy	6th Grade Math Standards – Adv/Reg Level	Pre-Algebra	Algebra/Math I	Geometry/Math II *Standardized Access to High Level Math and Associated Outcomes*
			7th Grade Math Standards	8th Grade Math Standards	Algebra/Math I
					Pre-Algebra

Table 5.3. Course-taking trajectories after Algebra I/Math I made available in seventh grade. No policy was in place that addressed the new advanced trajectory of courses. Furthermore, schools without teachers designated to teach "gifted" students did not offer the fifth/sixth "Compacted" Math course required to have access to Algebra/Math I in the seventh grade. The Cases of Alexander and Laila (described later in this chapter) are placed according to their situations within these course trajectories.

The Case of Alexander

Now enter Alexander, the protagonist of our first story and a fifth grade student. Alexander was being considered for the Compacted 5/6 math program in his school (see table 5.3). At Alexander's school, students were identified and their qualifications assessed by school personnel. Select students were also interviewed without knowing themselves why they were subjected to such scrutiny. After the process was completed, the school officials decided who would be admitted into the Compacted 5/6 math classes. Pursuant to the interview, Alexander realized that he was being considered for "an advanced math program." He later learned that he was not admitted into the program.

Alexander was disappointed. After all, mathematics was his favorite subject, and he had done quite well in all his math classes every year. So, without telling his parents, Alexander made an appointment with the school principal to ask whether there was anything he could do to participate in the new mathematics class. He just knew he would enjoy it and would do well if given the opportunity. To his amazement, the principal thought he was "out of line" for making such an inquiry and telephoned Alexander's parents to tell them so.

The telephone call from the principal was the first time Alexander's parents had heard anything about such a math class and their son's interest in it. Perhaps to the principal's surprise, Alexander's parents asked about the Compacted 5/6 course and wanted to know why their son could not be admitted. To be sure, they were aware of Alexander's interest in mathematics and his past success in the subject. Even so, they were told, flatly, that Alexander could not be placed in the course.

Being active members of a church that had an education committee to assist parents with understanding the education issues affecting their children, Alexander's parents asked the committee's chair, Martin, for help. Martin, a former mathematics teacher, telephoned someone he knew in the school district's central office who was in charge of elementary and middle school mathematics programs. Martin explained Alexander's situation and also expressed his concern that the new Compacted 5/6 and Compacted 6/7 configurations would have the effect of maintaining inequities in access to quality mathematics programs, in contradiction to the spirit of the school board policy that declared all students who met the stated criteria should have access to eighth grade algebra.

The district official, Joan, stated that "profoundly gifted" students must be placed ahead of "normal" students and, as such, the compacted approach was necessary. But this explanation contradicted the reality that only some elementary schools provided this "necessary" approach, whereas others did not even have the resources to offer the Compacted 5/6 class.

Joan concluded that Alexander should be denied access to the Compacted 5/6 math course at his school.

Undaunted, Martin made an appointment with Alexander's principal and the Compacted 5/6 mathematics teacher to advocate for Alexander's inclusion in the class. At the meeting were a number of supporters of Alexander's request, including his parents, Martin, and a tutor who would help Alexander if needed. Representing the school were the principal, the math teacher of the Compacted 5/6 course, and the district official, Joan, with whom Martin had spoken.

In the meeting, Martin explained Alexander was a good fit for the Compacted 5/6 mathematics course. Conversely, Joan presented some of Alexander's work that had not been completely exemplary. Specifically, the work Joan offered demonstrated that Alexander had not earned A+ marks. According to Joan, this was suggestive that Alexander did not merit being placed in the compacted course.

Martin argued that Alexander's work merited his placement into the compacted math course given that his report cards, end-of-grade scores, and objective performance data were all compatible with such a placement. Furthermore, Alexander had himself previously been identified as gifted. Martin explained that the turnout at the meeting itself was evidence that Alexander had the type of support that would ensure his success in the compacted course. Despite his efforts, Martin's arguments were rejected by Joan who reiterated her original claim that, while identified as gifted, Alexander was not "profoundly gifted."[6]

Over the objections of his parents and Martin, the school officials decided that Alexander should join the meeting. One school official expressed that Alexander needed to see how many adults were engaged in this "needless" effort to include him in a mathematics course. Martin, concerned about Alexander's becoming overwhelmed, insisted that no one speak with Alexander except Martin himself.

When Alexander arrived, he was shocked to see his parents, his grandmother, and Martin in the principal's office. Martin asked Alexander whether he knew why everyone was there. Alexander answered no. But his eyes lit brightly when Martin said that everyone was there because they cared about his education and were there to see about his getting into the math class he wanted. When the math teacher asked, "Do you realize that you are missing recess right now?" Alexander replied, "I'd miss all my recesses for a chance to be in that math class!"

After Alexander left, Joan turned to the principal and volunteered to make the final decision about admitting Alexander into the class, despite the fact that making the decision was the principal's responsibility. At this point, Martin turned to the principal and insisted that the decision be made *by the principal* and not relegated to others! The principal, feeling the pressure that

Martin exacted pursuant to the two of them belonging to the same church community, agreed to allow Alexander to take the class.

Alexander was quite pleased to be admitted into the class. His supporters were equally pleased and committed to helping him be successful. Consequently, members of Alexander's support network met once a month with his Compact 5/6 math teacher to monitor and discuss the actions of the teacher. This was done because there was a concern that the teacher might contribute to Alexander's failure to demonstrate that he should not have been placed in the class. Alexander's tutor remained available to help him, but Alexander didn't need any assistance.

At the same time, during the first few months, the teacher shared Alexander's work with his supporters and pointed out things that Alexander had done wrong. She voiced that this was evidence that he should not be in the class. On inspection, in each case, Martin, a math teacher himself, demonstrated that Alexander's errors were very minor and of little consequence.

As the quarters passed, by midyear, Alexander had distinguished himself as the top student in the class. Moreover, the teacher grew to identify him as an outstanding student, one who was likeable and willing to help others in the class. By the end of the year, Alexander had earned an A for the class. At the final meeting between Alexander's supporters and the school officials (including his Compact 5/6 math teacher), Alexander was described as a "wonderful student" who excelled.

When Martin asked the Compact 5/6 teacher and other school officials in attendance what we can learn from Alexander's case, they offered no immediate response. Martin waited and then suggested that "Maybe, we might be wrong about what students can do and what classes they should have access to." The Compact 5/6 math teacher countered by saying, "No! That's not the lesson here." She stated that Alexander was a different student than the one they had originally refused admission to. Further, she argued that Alexander had friends who sometimes got into trouble and that he hadn't always worked hard to succeed. "He's a different kid, now!" Then, she added that they would still keep the "old Alexander" from taking the class.

Martin couldn't believe what he had heard. He then realized that there were many more students needing an advocate to guarantee that they too would at least have access to opportunities to receive fair and equitable treatment in school. With that as his goal, Martin continued to work on behalf of students in that urban school district.

It's worth noting that Alexander was a young Black student who simply wanted to gain access to a subject that he enjoyed. Without academic evidence to the contrary, teachers ignored his past performance in math classes and relied instead on their own biases to inform their decisions about his capabilities. Put another way, the educators spurned a checklist-type measure put in place for equitable access to mathematics opportunity in favor of their belief story regarding a student. The educators' own beliefs clearly affected their responses to data. Then, those same beliefs affected the retrospective stories they told themselves to validate (and justify) their initial actions.

Given the opportunity to study high-quality mathematics, Alexander went on to middle school, where he enrolled in the new top track that was initiated by his journey in fifth grade. Alexander succeeded in his new middle school environment. Indeed, Alexander went on to high school and excelled in both academics and sports. Upon completion, he accepted a football scholarship at an Ivy League university.

The Case of Laila

A few years following the case of Alexander, Martin was again asked to provide support for a middle grades student whom we shall call Laila. In the same urban school district, Laila was denied access to eighth grade algebra. Laila's journey is telling because it relates to both teacher decision-making and teacher support of student success.

Laila took seventh grade pre-algebra and received a grade of A-. The objective predictive measures of performance that the school district used, including end-of-grade tests and Education Value-Added Assessment System (EVAAS)[7] for 3–12 scores were all high; they indicated that Laila should take algebra in the eighth grade. However, her seventh grade math teacher did not recommend her for eighth grade algebra despite her meeting the requirements of the school board policy (stated earlier) and Laila's success in math class. Although Laila and her mother indicated that Laila wanted to take eighth grade algebra because of her plans to attend college, Laila's request was denied (see table 5.3). Her math teacher, with school official support, explained that, because Laila "had to work hard for her high grades," she would not do well in the top-track eighth grade algebra class. It was further explained that such classes were for "naturals"—students who do not have to work hard to maintain good grades.

At this point, Laila's mother sought additional support. Aware of the work Martin did on behalf of students, she decided to ask for his help. Initially, she was a little embarrassed to ask because, as a professional woman, her perception was that she should be able to manage the situation by herself. Yet she had repeatedly spoken with teachers and the principal to no avail. She knew something else needed to be done.

Martin suggested that Laila's mother request a personalized education plan (PEP) that would create a template for how the school would provide extra help for Laila. With completed forms in hand, Martin, Laila, and Laila's mother met with Laila's teachers and the principal. The meeting began with Laila's math teacher stating that Laila's mother should be happy because, given Laila's background, Laila had achieved much more than would be expected. Laila's mother was livid! So Martin engaged the school officials during the meeting. Eventually, it was decided that Laila would be allowed to take eighth grade algebra. During the same time frame in this particular district, eighth grade algebra became a course that addressed both algebra and geometry and was now known as Math I.

In an effort to support Laila, Martin arranged for her to have a tutor. The tutor encouraged Laila to do her best and gave her extra work at times to fortify Laila's understanding of the mathematics. Unfortunately, the tutor and her mother felt that Laila was not supported by her teacher. One example of this is shared here.

Early in the class, students were asked to complete a project in which each student was asked to prepare a PowerPoint presentation to the school board about the cost of buying paper. In the presentation, a recommendation, based on the mathematics, would be made about what paper to buy. Laila completed the project and got it reviewed by her tutor. On review, the tutor felt the project was good and encouraged Laila to do the extra credit part as well, which she did. Laila got an F on the project.

The tutor showed the project to Martin to get his assessment. Martin felt the project work to be mathematically sound and otherwise typical for Laila's peer group. When Martin asked the teacher about the grade given to the project, he was told that "although the work was perfectly fine and correct, it was not captivating or compelling in its presentation."

Pursuant to this exchange between Martin and the math teacher, Laila's projects and tests were no longer returned to her. This meant Laila's work was not available for any adult in her life outside of school to examine. In short, this blocked access to Laila's support team and hindered their ability to assess the quality of Laila's work and progress in the course. Laila was informed only of her grades on class assignments. Finding this unacceptable, Martin worked to revise Laila's PEP in which it was explicitly stated that, subsequent to the teacher's evaluation, Laila's assignments must be returned to her for review.

For the entire school year, math class was "a nightmare" for Laila. The teacher refused to accept that Laila should have been placed in her class. And although Laila was performing well in class, the teacher expressed resentment that someone who wasn't a "natural" was allowed to take the course. At the end of the school year, before taking the Algebra/Math I End-of-Course (EOC) exam, which counted for 20% of her final grade, Laila had a B in the class. After completing the standardized End-of-Course test, which she aced, Laila received an A- in Algebra/Math I. But, unbelievably, her math teacher recommended that she repeat Math I as Math IA and Math IB in high school.[8]

Laila and her mother had hoped that Laila would be placed in Honors Math II in high school. But the "system" was not designed to affirm the work of students like Laila. In particular, students who did not make a "high" A in eighth grade Algebra/Math I were placed in Math I Foundations and Math IB in high school along with students who did not take eighth grade Algebra/Math I at all.

Upon investigation, Martin discovered that many high schools in this urban school district offered only remedial versions of Math I in high school, thus forcing students like Laila to retake Math I at a level below what they studied in eighth grade. Martin went to the central office to meet with the heads of the high school curriculum and the middle school math programs. They were not aware that many high schools were offering *only* remedial versions of Math I. After these officials checked for themselves, they confirmed what Martin had informed them about Math I in high school.

These officials also realized that many middle schools were recommending for Math II in ninth grade only those students who received a "high" A in Math I. As a consequence, these placement procedures and uneven opportunities resulted in "derailing" students. Those who took Math I in eighth grade pursuant to the new school board policy (cited above) did not benefit from the implementation of that policy because the policy did not cover high school placements. Taking Algebra/Math I in eighth grade ceases to be an opportunity when future course placements are effectively blocked.

Not all tales have a happy ending. Laila was initially placed into the remedial ninth grade Math I Foundations course. And, although the high school principal agreed to take Laila out of the Math I Foundations course and put her into Math II, the decision was made too late in the semester for her to actually enroll in the Math II course. She didn't take any math course during her freshman year. Dissatisfied with their daughter's treatment, Laila's parents enrolled her into a private school. Martin pursued the issue of placing eighth grade Math I students into ninth grade remedial Math I courses, but the school district refused to make the necessary changes to address the abuses of this procedure.

The Case of Inconsistent Leadership

Earlier in this chapter and in chapter 2, we referred to 103 sixth grade students who were overlooked for the top track in mathematics in a large urban middle school (see table 5.2). These students subsequently demonstrated their ability to be successful without any extraordinary interventions put into place. Critically, even though many of these students were previously designated as low-achieving or behaviorally and emotionally handicapped, they were placed into the top track because the principal of the school insisted that school board policy be followed and that these students be given an opportunity to succeed.

The principal's placement of these students (students who met the placement criteria for admittance into the class) met pushback from the mathematics faculty who were not in agreement with the principal's actions. In spite of the pushback, the students did well. An entire new pool of high-performing students was identified within the school.

These students performed well when given the opportunity to succeed. Indeed, three quarters of the students earned an A or B, and all but a few of the rest earned a C in the high-level mathematics course for which they qualified (figure 5.1). The data, in other words, would imply that the practice of following the academic guidelines was a success.

Nevertheless, when the principal was reassigned the next year to a high school, the mathematics faculty reverted back to old behaviors. During the next year, without the checklist in place (which simply assured placements were made following school board policy), students were similarly adjusted out of their proper placement.

Rather than addressing this disregard for school policy, the new principal acquiesced. He demonstrated unwillingness to contradict the sentiments of a mathematics faculty for the principle of equitable class placement. The faculty did not agree with extending opportunities to all students who met the school district's criteria for advanced placements. It did not matter that the data seen demonstrated that children meeting the school district's criteria were successful the year before. This evidence was not enough to get teachers and administrators to change their stories about, and their professional

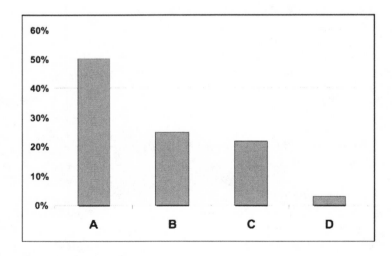

Figure 5.1.   First Semester Grades for the 103 Overlooked Students Enrolled in the Top-Track Sixth Grade Mathematics Course

evaluation of, Black and Latino children (the preponderance of students affected negatively by the old practices). Keeping in mind the three case studies above, in the next section we zoom out just a bit to consider the interplay of these student-level decisions and larger-system decisions.

CUMULATIVE IMPACT

Recall the study discussed in chapter 2 regarding the placement of young students into gifted programming. After determining that using teacher recommendations and parent requests led to racially biased outcomes for inclusion into gifted programs, a school district adopted a policy to screen everyone using more objective performance criteria for admission into the referral pool for gifted programs.[9] As a result, the racially biased placement patterns, seen previously in the district, were largely eliminated. What's more, student achievement and performance improved across student demographics.

However, in the face of these positive outcomes, the school district later claimed that the screening process was too expensive. They then reverted to the referral-based system that relies upon teacher and parent recommendations. Without the objective screening policy in place, racially biased student performance outcomes resurfaced—achievement and performance gaps returned to "normal."

How can this happen? We suggest that educators were unswayed and effectively unaffected by academic data that contradicted their prior beliefs about who should gain access to high-level academics. They resisted the data—even when it was demonstrated to have large cumulative impact.

In this way, the *individual* beliefs, attitudes, and dispositions surrounding decisions made about how students should be provided the opportunity to study rigorous mathematics has a *systemic* effect. When beliefs, attitudes, and dispositions are examined with the perspective of performance data and existing practices, the results reveal biases that inhibit ethnoracial minority and low-income students' access to high-quality content and instruction. Although many teachers and administrators have some awareness of such inequities, they seldom acknowledge the true magnitude of the problem or see their own role in it.

DATA VERSUS BELIEFS

Cultural beliefs and attitudes about low-income and ethnoracial minority students play a significant role in how students are placed in mathematics courses.[10] The use of performance data and objective achievement criteria helps educators avoid the unintentional (and intentional) biases students face.[11] Although many schools claim to use objective achievement criteria for making student placement decisions, more often than not, they use the data-driven approach—with adjustments.

Patrick Akos and his colleagues have consistently found that middle grade students appear to be "inequitably distributed among hierarchies of mathematics courses on the basis of race and economic background."[12, 13] Such disparities contribute to the ever-growing stratification among course opportunities for students. Similar results are found for high school students.[14] Specifically, even when academic achievement is comparable, Black and Hispanic students have less opportunity to take high-quality courses than their Asian and White counterparts. How does this happen? What decisions are made that continue to produce these inequitable results? Do beliefs trump data when data does not match prior beliefs?

Consider the large urban school district in which the cases of both Alexander and Laila occurred. Soon after implementation of the open-placement, data-driven opportunity protocol was put in place, the district argued that the use of objective performance data harmed ethnoracial minority students and girls. In particular, they argued that using the 70% likelihood-of-success cutoff score on the EVAAS measure resulted in more *unsuccessful* outcomes for students than they deemed appropriate, thereby suggesting that such students should be required to take remedial classes.[15]

It is certainly possible that educator resistance may have played a part here. The increase in "browner" and poorer students into classes that were formerly populated by the more affluent, as well as White and Asian American students, caused a kerfuffle in schools. Talk was about the increase in students identified as qualified for the highest-level math classes. While many teachers embraced the broader range of students in their classes, many others did not. For instance, a middle school math teacher (from a different school within the same time period) said to one of the authors here, "I don't know how to teach these children." This can be a vulnerable thing for a teacher to say. But it is also a bit confusing. "These children" demonstrated average or above-average performance for several years as evidenced by their EVAAS scores.

Nevertheless, the data indicated that a 70% predication-rate-of-success cutoff score created problems. Many students were not performing as well as expected and there was a racial and gender-based trend to the data. Girls and students of color did not perform as well as hoped. It makes good sense to question and reconsider this entrance policy. But 70% was not a magic number. The cutoff scores had a range of predictions from 0%–100%.

The same data that indicated to the district that some students (girls and students of color) were academically harmed by a 70% cutoff policy also demonstrated another phenomenon. A cutoff score of 80% likelihood of success resulted in more equitable placements than the status quo *and* had the desired student performance outcomes for Black and Hispanic students and girls. The data, in other words, indicated that a slight change in cutoff score *eliminated* the concern found at the initial cutoff score *and* produced more equitable placement results than did prior practice. Rather than modulate the cutoff scores based on equity and academic success, the system chose to end the use of objective performance data for placement purposes.

THE PATH OF MOST RESISTANCE

Explicit efforts within a school community to provide access to high-quality mathematics coursework has not proven to be easy or self-evident for the professionals involved. Efforts of educators and the pressures from some community members often hold steady to the tiered-opportunity model. Then, at the same time, students who qualify for these high-level opportunities often meet both unintentional and intentional resistance from teachers, counselors, and administrators.

Within the tiered-opportunity model, unintentional resistance and subsequent barriers can be identified and addressed. For instance, a school may identify an underrepresentation of girls (of all backgrounds) selected for the science team or of Black students recommended for the highest math courses.

Once a problem of this nature is identified, educators can use objective performance data to identify underrepresented students. This use of data supports educators in maintaining a high quality of professional judgment. Using this objective data also protects students from the damaging impact of prior belief when it comes to academic opportunity. From there educators can then address enhanced pedagogical approaches to teaching and learning as they strive to improve mathematics instruction along with opportunity.

The reality tends to look a little different. Keep in mind the conditions and demands faced by teachers as discussed in chapter 3. Change within this context can be difficult. This includes change that requires an understanding of issues such as implicit biases and student learning. And so, although educators are initially willing to try new approaches to the problem, teachers often balk at procedural and instructional solutions that demand significant changes in their own beliefs and behaviors.

It should not be surprising that efforts for equitable access to high-quality opportunity has proven a formidable task.[16] Educators and the school districts that they run often possess deeply held beliefs and attitudes about intelligence, racial differences, social class, privilege, and entitlements that affect student access to high-quality instruction.[17] Educators involved in school mandates that provide tiered opportunities, such as gifted and talented programs, have a stake in maintaining the status quo and the philosophies surrounding that status quo. This may mean that any changes in school practices and policies are resisted. Moreover, affluent parents often exercise their status by voicing concerns about equitable policies they fear will eliminate privileged placements for their children.[18]

Ultimately, reactions to equitable student opportunity can quickly come to function as intentional resistance even though it is often unacknowledged. Intentional resistance, as we have witnessed it in the school setting, manifests as a pattern of ignoring objective achievement data and proven pedagogical approaches to student success. We've experienced educators acknowledging that new pedagogical strategies may work for students they've identified for placement into advanced courses. At the same time, these same educators may be convinced that these new, proven strategies will not be successful with those students thought to be incapable of performing well in rigorous math courses. The cases of Alexander, Laila, and Inconsistent Leadership, chronicled above, serve as examples of this phenomenon.

As we will discuss further in the next chapter, placement policies about providing access to high-quality courses and instruction should not vary by year, or by school, or by leadership in any given school district. Each school district should create policies and procedures that meet the needs of all students and are fully understood and consistently implemented by school officials.

We have so far considered how the data-driven ethic has some problems from the perspective of enactment. Beliefs bump up against data. A disregard for protocol may ensue. We will look further at the idea of the belief story and how it affects the interpretation of data in chapter 6. For now, note that data does not tend to trigger actions or shape beliefs. In other words, beliefs drive people's relationship to data and not the other way around. Given this, let's consider how beliefs might arise in the professional work of teaching. In particular, what might it look like to have a belief interrupted so that the academic data has a chance to be seen?

In chapter 6, we consider the human side of processing data and proffer a set of solutions to the questions we have raised. Once individuals understand that beliefs are what drive interpretations of data, then a corollary presents itself. Seeing how data gets interpreted demands seeing one's own beliefs. What's more, seeing one's own beliefs demands questions be raised about equity, parity, and intention.

NOTES

1. Note that these cases are neither unique nor unusual. The authors, who have extensive experience within public schools, have chosen but a few of the many meetings and interactions that illuminate the relationship between math, race, bias, and opportunity in schools. We have chosen instances that are well documented by data, notes, and memory.

2. Only very isolated school districts in the United States offer rigorous mathematics to all as a policy through middle school. Most recently, San Francisco United School District has

eliminated tracking in eighth grade and mandates that *all* students take algebra in ninth grade and not in middle school. See Sawchuk, S. (2018, June 12). A bold effort to end algebra tracking shows promise. Retrieved from https://www.edweek.org/ew/articles/2018/06/13/a-bold-effort-to-de-track-algebra-shows.html.

3. See, for instance, Hallinan (2003) for a display of academic performance versus actual placement in a large data set of high school students. Hallinan, M. T. (2003). Ability grouping and student learning. Brookings Papers on Education Policy. Washington, DC: Brookings Institution Press.

4. In this district, end-of-grade assessments are on a 5-point (V) scale.

5. Hoffer, T. B., Rasinski, K. A., & Moore, W. (1995). *Social background differences in high school mathematics and science coursetaking and achievement* (NCES 95-206). National Center for Education Statistics. Washington, DC: U.S. Department of Education; Gutierrez, R. (2000). Advancing African American, urban youth in mathematics: Unpacking the success of one math department. *American Journal of Education, 109*(1), 63–111; The Education Trust–West. (2004). *The A–G curriculum:* College-prep? Work-prep? Life prep: Understanding and implementing a rigorous core curriculum for all. Oakland, CA: Author. Retrieved from https://west.edtrust.org/wp-content/uploads/sites/3/2015/02/College-Prep-Work-Prep-Life-Prep.pdf; Garrity, D. (2004). Detracking with vigilance: By opening the high-level doors to all, Rockville Centre closes the gap in achievement and diplomas. *School Administrator, 61*(7), 24–27; The Education Trust. (2005). *Gaining traction, gaining ground: How some high schools accelerate learning for struggling students.* Washington, DC: Author. Retrieved from https://edtrust.org/wp-content/uploads/2013/10/GainingTractionGainingGround.pdf; and Burris, C. C., Heubert, J. P., & Levin, H. M. (2006). Accelerating mathematics achievement using heterogeneous grouping. *American Educational Research Journal, 43*(1), 105–136.

6. To be clear, "profoundly gifted" is not a recognized category used to describe or identify students either generally in schools or within this school system.

7. EVAAS is a customized software system developed by SAS Analytics and available to school districts. EVAAS examines the impact of teachers, schools, and districts on the learning of their students in specific courses, grades, and subjects. Users can access information that predicts student success, shows the effects of schooling at particular schools, or reveals patterns in subgroup performance.

8. If this is not jarring to you, consider this. Laila received an A- in Math I (which is considered an honors course when taken in a middle school setting). Given her A- grade, this would logically imply that Laila proceed to the next honors course in the sequence, Honors Math II. A step below that would be a recommendation for Math II. Math II is not entirely logical, but it would at least not deny Laila access to new content. The step below, in this tiered approach, would be Math I. This would be a one semester repeat of the content for which she just received an A-. The next step below—the course sequence for which Laila was recommended—would be a repeat of Math I content over the course of two semesters. The only recommendation below that in general education would be pre-algebra, where Laila would go back to content that is taught before Math I. And if you thought to yourself, *well, still, maybe the teacher saw something that the data did not*, we hope you notice that this thought must be driven by some belief, for it is not driven by the data of Laila's performance.

9. Card, D., & Giuliano, L. (2015). *Can universal screening increase the representation of low income and minority students in gifted education?* (No. w21519). National Bureau of Economic Research. See also a report on and expansion of the implications of this study in Dynarski, S. (2016, April 10). Why talented Black and Hispanic students can go undiscovered. *New York Times,* p. BU6.

10. Mayer, A. (2008). Understanding how U.S. secondary schools sort students for instructional purposes: Are all students being served equally? *American Secondary Education, 36*(2), 7–25.

11. Stiff, L. V., & Johnson, J. L. (2011). Mathematical reasoning and sense making begins with the opportunity to learn. In M. E. Strutchens & J. R. Quander (Eds.), *Focus in high school mathematics: Fostering reasoning and sense making for all students* (pp. 85–100). Reston, VA: National Council of Teachers of Mathematics.

Chapter 5

12. Akos, P., Shoffner, M., & Ellis, M. (2007). Mathematics placement and the transition to middle school. *Professional School Counseling, 10*(3), 238–244.

13. Grissom, J. A., & Redding, C. (2016). Discretion and disproportionality: Explaining the underrepresentation of high-achieving students of color in gifted programs. *AERA Online, 2*(1), 1–15.

14. Mayer, A. (2008). Understanding how U.S. secondary schools sort students for instructional purposes: Are all students being served equally? *American Secondary Education, 36*(2), 7–25.

15. As well as the firsthand experience of the authors, a citation is also available here. It is not provided in order to maintain school district confidentiality throughout this chapter.

16. There are documented examples of schools that have held steady to data, disbanded leveled opportunities, and made a difference in student school experiences and opportunity. These cases continue to be the exception and not the norm. See, for instance, Burris, C. C., Heubert, J. P., & Levin, H. M. (2006). Accelerating mathematics achievement using heterogeneous grouping. *American Educational Research Journal, 43*(1), 105–136; and Boaler, J. (2006). How a detracked mathematics approach promoted respect, responsibility, and high achievement. *Theory into Practice, 45*(1), 40–46.

17. Oakes, J., & Wells, A. S. (1998). Detracking for high student achievement. *Education Leadership, 55*(6), 38–41.

18. McGrath, D. J., & Kuriloff, P. J. (1999). "They're going to tear the doors off this place": Upper-middle-class parent school involvement and the educational opportunities of other people's children. *Educational Policy, 13*(5), 603–629.

Chapter Six

Unpacking Belief and Finding Change

In this book we have told a story about how decisions made by conscientious and well-meaning individuals can adversely affect access and opportunity for others. We have shown the importance of data-driven decision-making in a range of professions and vocations. We have also illustrated how data that *should be* used to inform decision-making has been invoked and then sometimes used, sometimes argued with, and sometimes ignored. In short, irrespective of work setting, most individuals are not easily moved by data when engaging in the decision-making process.

And yet data can serve to ensure sounder decisions that result in better opportunities and fairer outcomes for those whose lives and future prospects will be affected. We believe the use of data in decision-making by teachers and other education professionals is especially critical because the decisions can (and often do) determine the fates of the children and youth touched by those decisions.

For this final chapter we explore, or unpack, the concept of "belief-stories." When unmonitored, the belief-stories individuals draw upon tend to operate unconsciously and in a fashion that undermines the use of data in decision-making.

We conclude this chapter with considerations toward finding the path to change. These considerations stem from the prominent questions we hope were provoked by the stories, ideas, data, and concerns that have arisen throughout this book. Through them we highlight how education professionals can begin to unpack some of the more prominent barriers that undermine diligent and consistent use of data-based decision-making in schools. Ultimately, we believe these considerations have direct implications for how teachers and other education professionals can realize the ideal of equitable decision-making in schools.

UNPACKING BELIEF: DATA AND THE BRAIN

In chapter 2 we considered several instances where data was used to affect decision-making and to reduce bias. These are success stories. Baseball teams adjusted their evaluation of baseball players, and doctors realigned their evaluation of patients, based on data that demonstrated the need to change. Moved by inequities, symphonies changed the way they auditioned musicians. Data then arose to support the merit of that decision and to reinforce the continued use of the practice. This seems so logical, and, indeed, these examples serve as models for engaging with data. At the same time, these examples are the exceptions, not the rule.

Data is an intoxicating story these days. Big data and data-driven decision-making are part of our vernacular. The story those phrases tell are, more or less, well known. Big data allows people to see trends in human behavior; it allows them to predict behaviors and is a part of everyday life.

Data-driven decision-making is an idea, even an ethic, that decisions should be made with objective data whenever possible. That's the story. Unfortunately, this story is less like nonfiction and more like a fable.

A fundamental idea behind data-driven decision-making is that people will use and respond to data in a predictable fashion. When someone is presented with data, so the story goes, that data will inform and affect that person's understandings, decisions, and beliefs. A belief story plus data will morph into a new story and set of actions that were affected by that data. In this scenario, people's beliefs are fluid enough that data matters. In fact, you would probably agree that the moral of the data-driven decision-making story is that *data* will drive people to a better decision than will their beliefs alone.

In *The Influential Mind: What the Brain Reveals about Our Power to Change Others*, the cognitive neuropsychologist Tali Sharot outlines the neuropsychological and behavioral evidence for how data actually affects beliefs and behaviors. As noted below, Sharot summarizes the quandary that exists at the nexus of data, the brain, human beliefs, and behavior:

> So you can imagine my dismay when I learned that all those numbers, from numerous experiments and observations, pointed to the fact that people are not in fact driven by facts, or figures, or data. It is not that people are stupid; nor are we ridiculously stubborn. It is that the accessibility to lots of data, analytic tools, and powerful computers is the product of the last few decades, while the brains we are attempting to influence are the product of millions of decades. As it turns out, while we adore data, the currency by which our brains assess said data and make decisions is very different from the currency many of us believe our brains should use. The problem with an approach that prioritizes information and logic is that it ignores the core of what makes you and me human: our motives, our fears, our hopes and desires. [1]

Sharot continues by describing how established beliefs are resistant to change even, and perhaps especially, in the face of evidence provided to shake up or undermine those beliefs. In other words, our initial belief stories are very resistant to change.[2]

Confirmation Bias

One demonstration of the persistence of a given belief story, as summarized by Sharot, is that of people's response to arguments for or against the death penalty. The researchers Charles Lord, Lee Ross, and Mark Lepper presented people with two fabricated studies regarding the death penalty. The participants were to analyze the studies and decide whether the studies were convincing. What the investigators found was that believers in the death penalty saw the study supporting the death penalty (we will call it study 1) to be convincing and that the study itself was well constructed. These same believers in the death penalty evaluated the study contradictory to their own beliefs (study 2) to be poorly constructed and unconvincing.

The against-the-death-penalty believers had exactly the same reactions but in the opposite direction. Against-the-death-penalty participants found study 1 to be unconvincing and poorly constructed and study 2, to be convincing and well constructed.

The key here is that, after reviewing the studies, each group found the data that supported their own belief story to be valuable and the data that did not support their belief story as unfounded or less convincing. Data, then, did not affect their prior beliefs. On the other hand, their belief stories did affect their interpretation of the data.[3]

Indeed, Sharot concludes that human response to data can, and usually does, have the effect of reinforcing and heightening the original belief and story held by the individual. Overall, she concludes, data can have a polarizing effect because people pick and choose data to reinforce their own beliefs. She notes, "[i]n fact, presenting people with information that contradicts their opinion can cause them to come up with altogether new counterarguments that further strengthen the original view."[4] This confirmation bias is "one of the strongest biases humans hold."[5]

Sharot also reports on two other findings connected to confirmation bias. First, the tendency to be affected by confirmation bias may actually be stronger in people who are more analytical. Even ability within the realm of statistics and mathematics does not provide protection from this phenomenon. Indeed, those with an analytical strength appear even more vulnerable to the effects of confirmation bias when interpreting data because they can twist the arguments and evidence toward their own view.

Second, there is evidence that brain activity is reduced when a past decision is contradicted and elevated when a past decision is confirmed. In other words, even at a neuropsychological level, people appear to *tune out* information that *does not fit* their prior decisions and the beliefs that inspired those decisions. On the other hand, people's brains light up when their ideas are somehow confirmed.[6]

Recall the extended Sharot quote above and the idea that humans aren't compelled by data. What about the tail end of this quote that references the emotional side of being human?

> The problem with an approach that prioritizes information and logic is that it ignores the core of what makes you and me human: our motives, our fears, our hopes and desires. (p. 14)

To consider this human side of the story, we will turn to Kathryn Schulz and her work on the woes and joys of *Being Wrong*.[7] Specifically, we will look at motives, fears, hopes, and desires by considering certainty, doubt, and the exquisitely human need to confabulate.

Certainty, Doubt, and Confabulation

Let's think first about certainty and doubt from the perspective of feelings. How does certainty feel? Certainty, as described by Schulz, is biologically necessary in humans. Without certainty, people might never take action or move through the world with a sense of ease. Considering the evolutionary utility of certainty, Schulz explains that "[i]n a practical sense, . . . it's clear that we sometimes behave as if a proposition is true before we have had a chance to evaluate it."[8] Humans have to be certain about some things in order to function. The bottom line of certainty is that it keeps people moving through the world and it feels good.

At the same time, certainty is different from knowledge. Knowledge is complex and involves inquisition and the evolution of ideas. You might even say that knowledge requires the investigation of confusions and doubts. Knowledge is messy. Certainty is not. Moreover, certainty appears to neurologically reinforce itself. In addition to certainty, feeling neurologically good by ensuring that past decisions are confirmed, it also reduces neurological engagement when faced with a contradiction.

But the simplicity of certainty has a downside. While biologically necessary, certainty is "lethal to two of our most redeeming and humane qualities, imagination and empathy."[9] Certainty steamrolls over nuance and doubt.

How does doubt feel? Schulz summarizes it like this: "Where certainty reassures us with answers, doubt confronts us with questions, not only about our future but also about our past: about the decisions we made, the beliefs we held . . . the very way we lived our lives."[10]

How do people take in a vast and complicated world, filled with doubt, and create enough certainty to move forward with decisiveness and a sense of precision? They do it by structuring the world with the stories they tell.

The vast language-based human brain is wired to tell stories. Telling stories is a most fantastic of all assets for humans. Imagination and stories allow people to do the glorious and human things we do, like developing cures for illnesses, remembering loved ones who cease to exist, communicating ideas through a book, or creating engaging and effective classroom environments. At the same time, stories, ideas, conjectures, and imaginations all involve inference. And inference, by definition, implies a space between facts and conclusions.[11] Humans fill that space all the time. Get in your car and take a drive, and you will see for yourself as you fill that space freely with stories flung from your imagination.

> *Why would he walk into the crosswalk with six seconds left? He won't get all the way across in six seconds . . . he's not even running. He must be one of those millennials who thinks the world revolves around him.*

Or:

> *You don't stop at a blinking yellow, you doof. Didn't you take driver's ed? I see those license plates, yeah, they don't know how to drive there.*

Or perhaps more generously:

> *I am glad I was awesome and stopped at this crosswalk. I think I made that woman with the heavy bags really happy. She is clearly tired and wants to get home. Probably getting home to cook dinner for her kids.*

You can try to stop doing this, but you just can't. It is part of being human. Humans constantly process facts and data through the framework of stories.

Schulz describes this duality as the interworking of the storytelling and the fact-checking parts of the brain. The storyteller and the fact-checker. Because of the survival-level need to make inferences toward a level of certainty, the storyteller can quickly take over, leaving the fact-checker behind. Schulz identifies this phenomenon as confabulation.[12] Confabulating is, well, fabulous. It is that active storyteller filling in the gaps between data and conclusions. Confabulation is so quick that it's hard to interrupt. Often, even without the fact-checker's permission, the story gets written. Once written, confirmation bias protects the story from doubt.

Confabulation, which is merely the inferences made and the stories they form, can be subtle, like when someone is driving down the street taking in information or wondering what might have happened to a friend who is late.

It can be part of a day-to-day story you tell yourself about a neighbor you barely know or the celebrity you've never met.

Once people notice confabulation and see how it works, they can begin to unpack their thinking and the stories created to support that thinking. Notice in yourself how you fill in the structure with just a couple of sticks. For instance, you might explain why a particular business venture is destined to succeed or fail, why a neighbor you have never met got rid of their dog, or why a person is stopped on the side of the road as you drive by on the bus. We confabulate all the time.

New information, or data, will always be understood within the context of confabulations, inferences, stories, and beliefs. To maintain a stable and certain world, if data doesn't fit, the belief becomes good enough to be used as if it were data. The imaginary driver described above turned the irritating fact that someone walked into a crosswalk (with time left) into proof of a prior belief about a generation. Wow. What a leap.

UNPACKING BELIEF: AVAILABILITY BIAS AND ANCHORS

Another way to think about this phenomenon is through the lenses of both an availability heuristic and a tendency toward anchoring. In *Thinking, Fast and Slow*, Daniel Kahneman defines the availability bias as the process of judging frequency by "the ease with which instances come to mind" (p. 129).[13] Essentially, people making decisions tend to be affected by ideas and paradigms that are frequent and readily available to them.

The phenomenon of anchoring is the tendency of humans to orient their understandings around a previously provided piece of information. So, if one is provided a number or percentage regarding a certain situation, his estimates about even unrelated situations will be affected by that previously provided number. We are arguing here that, in education, "the gap" is a *readily available anchor* that affects the stories many educators tell themselves about students, student placements, and existing inequities.

A NEW ANCHOR

Because of the propensity to allow beliefs to drive thoughts, conclusions, and decisions, it is important that decision-makers notice confabulations and the available anchors that inform them and to accept the imperfect way in which they draw conclusions. Even if data is brought to the table, the conclusions drawn are likely not as unbiased or objective as perhaps the cultural zeitgeist for data-driven decisions might imply. Most of the time, *people's stories* get in the way. And these stories are *driven by available anchors* accepted as truth in order to organize the world.

When considering the use of data, professionals must remember that there is a human side to integrating data. This human side—filled with fears, hopes, beliefs, doubts, anchors, and bias—matters. It matters, fundamentally, for at least two reasons. First, the practitioner faced with doubts becomes vulnerable, or perhaps defensive to this vulnerability, in a way that is not generally recognized, supported, or understood. This unaddressed, or unacknowledged, vulnerability can compromise professional decision-making and affect conversations.

The second reason the human side matters is that any compromise in professional decision-making stands to alter the hopes, beliefs, fears, doubts, and experiences of the people and students under our care. Indeed, compromised or unconsciously driven professional decision-making stands to negatively alter the results, the outcomes, and the very lives of those we are entrusted to serve.

It is important to create a new anchor for these decisions and conversations. This new anchor includes acknowledgment that inferences are imperfectly drawn. This new anchor reframes student performance as being *about* student performance and not about demographic background characteristics. This new anchor disrupts the idea of a gap and instead recognizes systemic differences in performance *as about the implementation of problematic systems* and not the children affected by these systems.

CULTURAL NORMS, RACE, AND BELIEF

The phenomenon of belief stories offers insights into why and how individuals will tend to use (or not use) data when engaging in decision-making. As teacher educators, however, our primary interest is in unpacking ways that belief stories and related phenomena influence the inclinations of education professionals *to not use* (or *to misinterpret*) pertinent data when making critical instructional placement decisions about students in classrooms and schools. More specifically, we are concerned with why peripheral information gets privileged *over and above* objective data and how such information figures in decisions that affect the quality of learning opportunities afforded children and youth from racial and ethnic minority backgrounds.

At its most fundamental, the concept of data-based decision-making in classrooms and schools is about education professionals demonstrating both the *will* and the *conviction* to make decisions that are in the best interest of students. It also means utilizing the data that is most directly relevant to the learning or instructional issue at hand. Lamentably, in many schools, the will and conviction we refer to here are not affecting decision-making in a meaningful way.

Indeed, we know of far too many cases where education professionals have made instructional and course placement decisions by drawing on information that was unrelated to the actual needs of given students. That is to say, the professionals disregarded relevant objective data and instead based their decisions on *peripheral and unrelated information* about the backgrounds of the students.

We have witnessed how such decision-making defied common sense and, in some circumstances, contradicted written school policies. Most troubling has been when the professionals' explanations for their decisions have belied their own claims of fairness and commitment to high-quality learning opportunities for all students. The *real-life cases* of Alexander and Laila, detailed in chapter 5 of this book, are just two examples of this type of egregiously compromised decision-making.

When faced with the highly consequential task of placing students for instruction (let's say, recommending a student for an advanced course of study), it seems only logical that education professionals would begin by *drawing on the most relevant and objective data.* Yet a growing body of scholarship (including our own) reveals that many education professionals are drawn instead to subjective anchors and peripheral information when making these types of critical decisions. This tendency is especially common when Black students are the targets of the decisions.

Belief stories highlight the effects of what can be thought of as the *psychological wiring* that predisposes some education professionals to not use the most pertinent data when making decisions involving Black children and youth. Whether they can recognize and then choose to ignore their belief stories, however, is linked to the professionals' own sociocultural mooring.

The notion of sociocultural mooring relates to the phenomenon of socialization, which, in some respects, begins before a person is born (think parents' selection of pink for girls and blue for boys) and continues throughout life. Still and all, it is during a person's formative years (childhood and adolescence) that the most enduring imprints of socialization are put into place. Sensoy and DiAngelo (2017) defined socialization as "the systematic training into the norms of our culture."[14]

Socialization as a process results from the vast collection of experiences, narratives, and images to which people are exposed. It begins in the family (most basic social unit) yet is added to and reinforced through interactions with friends, institutions (e.g., places of worship and schools), and mass media (e.g., advertising, magazines, radio, television, movies, music, and the internet). Through repeated direct and vicarious exposures, tremendous influence is exerted over how individuals think about, engage with, and react to the world around them.

One of the purest indicators of the power of socialization is apparent in the normal, automatic, and unscripted thoughts and related behaviors individuals have and display in relation to their interactions with other people. Seemingly innocuous thoughts and responses can be quite revealing (and consequential) when people encounter, interact with, and make decisions that affect those whom they perceive are different from themselves. This is especially the case when the difference is defined by race.

Historian George Frederickson (2002) traced how in the United States [15] race has been seen, treated, and even reified (through socialization, tradition, culture, and law) as a particularly distinctive marker of difference between and among groups. For many, race represents an essential or core feature of human diversity, with each group believed to be distinguishable from the others by unique and immutable traits and characteristics. While some diverse groups may be seen as having some similarities, other groups are perceived as possessing a degree of uniqueness that is theirs alone. The socialization (or sociocultural mooring) that gives rise to this line of thinking about race difference easily explains (and is often used to justify) "blink of the eye" [16] associations many people make with the race differences they encounter.

FINDING CHANGE

For the remaining sections of this chapter, we focus on recommendations or answers to issues embedded in belief stories and sociocultural moorings. These issues need to be unpacked for education professionals to begin to understand and work to remove the barriers that stand in the way of consistently sound, data-based decision-making practices in schools.

#1: Recognize Conceptual Race

Increasing diversity in the United States population means that the children and youth education professionals encounter in schools will come from many different backgrounds across an array of social axes, including, but not limited to, economic class, primary language, and religious beliefs. (See chapter 3 for a full discussion of this issue.) The historical and present-day realities of life in the United States reveal that the access to high-quality schooling made available to these students, for good or ill, will be based on a number of these axes. And the axis that will have an outsized impact will be *race*.

Have you ever wanted to ignore or become "color blind" to race? Many people do. Among education professionals, it is not uncommon for those who work with students whose racial backgrounds differ from their own to claim that they *do not see color* (race) among their students. But unless they have blindness, invariably educators can and do literally see the skin colors (a common proxy for race differences) among their students. So why do so many professionals feel compelled to make such an obviously *inaccurate* claim? Why would anyone desire not to be able to discern race differences?

It is likely that the desire to *not see color* arises from the fact that race is the single most angst-producing reality of life in the United States.[17] A cursory study of the nation's history makes plain how all manner of rights and opportunities (including high-quality schooling) have been afforded (and in other cases denied) to individuals and groups on the basis of race. Even in contemporary United States society, it is common for people engaged in everyday activities (e.g., future freshman visiting a college campus, a family barbecuing in the park, or an exhausted graduate student taking a nap while studying) to be subjected to indignities based on reactions others have to their race. Consequently, it's probable some education professionals claim they don't (or wish they didn't) see color because, like many people in the United States, they yearn for a time when *negative realities* linked to race will no longer exist. While, indeed, race is at once a construct that has been created and maintained by political and social policies throughout United States history,[18] it is, at the same time, a reality within United States culture. Race diversity and myriad unpleasant responses to this diversity is a fact of U.S. life.

So profoundly central is race to U.S. life that an analytic framework, critical race theory (CRT), is used by scholars in numerous academic and professional fields to study how race diversity "is deliberately exploited and/or subversively implicated in the perpetuation and entrenchment of systems of oppression . . . across various social realms . . . including the nation's schools."[19] Tensions attributed to race diversity gave rise to (and continue to nurture) the scourge that is *racism*, a complex form of oppression.

A basic precept of CRT is that racism is a *normal* part of U.S. life. This means racism is not atypical but rather is deeply woven into the very fabric of our culture. Its pervasiveness in the commonplace and mundane framing of people's lives allows racism to inform (and be performed in) ordinary, day-to-day interactions with family, friends, work associates, and others with whom people come into contact.

This means racism manifests not just as individual (deliberate or inadvertent) detrimental behaviors; it also encompasses economic, political, and social structures that define how people work and function in societal institutions, including schools. Understanding its multifaceted nature helps illuminate why racism is often imperceptible (or, when named, is explained away as something other than what it is) to all except those to whom its negative and dehumanizing effects are directed and experienced.

One of the more insidious manifestations of racism is its insinuation into common categories people draw upon in their everyday lives. Various writers have described this insinuation as occurring, usually inconspicuously, through the layered phenomenon of *conceptual* race. This is the coded, euphemistic, even genteel language people adopt and use that allows them to allude to race while not mentioning or naming it directly and outright. Ladson-Billings described it thusly,

> [O]ur conceptions of race . . . are more embedded and fixed than in a previous age. However, this embeddedness or "fixed-ness" has required new language and constructions of race so that denotations are submerged and hidden. . . . Conceptual categories like "school achievement," "middle classness," "maleness," "beauty," "intelligence," and "science" become normative categories for whiteness, while categories like "gangs," "welfare recipients," "basketball players," and "the underclass" become the marginalized and de-legitimated categories of blackness. [20]

Among the conceptual race categories common in schools are *academically gifted, at risk*, and *discipline problem*. We might also think of these categories as frequently used and available heuristics that guide our thinking and anchor our expectations. Scholars have detailed how these and other conceptual race categories affect all aspects of schooling, including teacher-student interpersonal interactions, behavior management protocols, and instructional placement decisions. [21]

The impacts of such categories go largely unchallenged because they are cloaked in nonracial language and employed by education professionals who often have a deeply held belief that they are themselves caring, fair, and color blind. This is to say, under normal circumstances in schools, professionals are likely to respond to race in ways that are largely reflexive or hidden to their own conscious thought. Consequently, the conceptual race categories used and associations made are likely to inform mundane as well as critical decisions they make about students unless effort is made to interrupt the process, the inferences, and the stories being told.

Having witnessed (and worked to counteract) so many instances and cases where conceptual race was being foregrounded in critical decision-making over students' actual abilities, we recognize that race often informs, or anchors, the thinking and work of education professionals in ways that seem instinctive. Yet making decisions based on irrelevant information is not instinctive at all. Instead, it is a learned behavior that through socialization is driven largely by what teacher education scholar Joyce King (1991) has described as "dysconsciousness." She explains this phenomenon as "an uncritical habit of mind (including perceptions, attitudes, assumptions, and beliefs) that justifies inequity and exploitation by accepting the existing order of things as given (p. 135)." [22]

Thus, this first recommendation is our answer to one of the more pernicious barriers to sound, data-based decision-making in classrooms and schools. It is the barrier of race and the associations most people in the United States make with the race (colors) that they see. We have observed how the race of African American students, in particular, often figures more prominently than objective data indicators of the students' actual demonstrated academic abilities in decision-making about instructional placements.

We call upon education professionals to jettison the wholly illogical claim of color blindness. In its place, we challenge them to interrogate the obscured conceptions and meanings that are subconsciously associated with the colors (races) they do see through conceptual notions of race. We challenge them to notice how these associations affect the stories they tell themselves about students. Ultimately, it is through awareness, will, and commitment to fairness that education professionals can unlearn such practices and adopt data-based decision-making.

#2 Free the Data, Free the Mind(set)

We speculate that, for far too many education professionals, the prospect of using data betrays a homogenized view of students of different backgrounds. We contend further that students are so often viewed through the lens of difference (reified by the achievement-gap mean as it supports ideas about conceptual "whiteness" and conceptual "blackness") that it has become a habit of mind. In general (the habit, or story, reminds us), Black students perform poorly compared to their White peers.

With gap-thinking and gap-based data interpretation, school districts accept patterns of advanced placement that reflect a status quo of opportunities gained or denied. How do educators move toward more accurate and equitable interpretations of student data? We seek to free the data to free the mind. Or, if you prefer, to free the mind to free the data. In either direction, the goal is to generate school- and community-wide discussions related to belief stories and interpreting data.

This book began by considering data in professional hockey and the reality that systems in place greatly advantage one arbitrary set of players over another. The story told about professional sports is that player selections are merit based. Great players rise to the top, and weak players are cut by meaningful evaluations of talent. But the hockey-gap data complicates that story. Two equally capable groups of players demonstrate consistently different overall achievement outcomes. Something other than merit must be at play.

In the case of hockey, an age-based early identification system and the implicit bias held for relatively older players combine to create substantial inequities of access and opportunity. This difference in access and opportunity leads to a difference in outcomes (vis-à-vis selection into the NHL). Specifically, the outcomes for one group (those children born late in the year) is unnaturally suppressed to the advantage of another (those born early in the year).

With regard to mathematics opportunities in schools, the structure is the same. A system that values early opportunity and differentiation of experience combines with implicit biases—belief stories—about which students are most capable of performing in an academic setting. This results in substantial inequities of access and opportunity. These inequities in opportunity create a difference in performance indicators.

And yet, reactions to these fundamentally similar phenomenon are quite different.[23] When interpreting what is known as the academic achievement gap, most educators we have worked with have a default understanding of the graph as describing an *expected and natural occurrence.* Natural in the sense that the gap describes the widely agreed upon problem that Black students don't perform as well as White students. Natural in the sense that it is not surprising. Natural in the sense that the graph quantifies and measures the agreed upon problem that needs to be addressed. That problem is the low performance of Black students.

When interpreting the hockey graph, most people immediately understand the gap in draft status as an *unexpected and unnatural occurrence.* Unnatural in the sense that the players themselves, regardless of their fundamental potentials and merit, *are caught in a trap that defines their outcomes based on an arbitrariness of birthdate.* The performance of the players is not the problem that needs to be addressed. Indeed, the differential performance of the players is evidence of a *different* problem *that points away* from the players themselves.

So why the difference in interpretation of hockey players versus children in schools? We contend that a *merit-based academic belief story (grounded in entrenched ideas about differences between groups based on race)* obscures the reality that the data of the gap describes an *unexpected and unnatural occurrence* wherein the students *are caught in a trap that restricts their outcomes based on unrelated demographic background characteristics.*

We contend that the gap is an unnatural occurrence resulting in large part from the systematic manipulation of student access, opportunity, and academic experience found in schools. We therefore suggest that educators engage with belief stories about educational access to disentangle *ideas about merit-based opportunity* from the *realities of who is provided opportunity* in their school community.

Related to this merit-based belief story is how it affects an individual's interpretation of the data on the big-picture or framework level. In our experience, most school personnel (and community members) conceptualize the gap, either implicitly or explicitly, as fundamentally *about student performance.* This conceptualization, this story, implies an interpretation of the data at the student level, and it goes like this: one set of students is not performing as well as another set of students. This is the gap-logic we described and discussed in chapter 4.

But there is another way to interpret that same data as fundamentally *about differential opportunity*. This conceptualization implies an interpretation of the data at the systems level. The gap then becomes evidence that an unnatural suppression of student performance disadvantages one group of students to the advantage of another. In this scenario, educators and community members understand that a consistent gap in achievement *is not how the data behaves in a population of students who are provided equitable access and opportunity.*

When the story changes and the data is understood at the systems level, the mission of the school community shifts away from helping poor performers or advancing high achievers. Instead, the mission becomes discovering which patterns and habits of practice contribute to the systematic suppression of student performance.

Furthermore, as educators and the larger school community engage in discussions about equitable opportunity, it is also important to consider the impact these unnaturally created stratifications have on the development of talent in the long run. When academic players are cut at a young age, the whole team suffers.

Considerations regarding effort and talent development complicate another belief story. In particular, understanding talent development as largely about sustained effort complicates the belief that identification of young talent is a meaningful and pertinent pursuit.

The widely held belief story found in the United States, that mathematics ability is largely an innate characteristic, serves to justify the practice of identifying young talent and providing differential experiences. But qualities manifest in youngsters do not necessarily speak to the qualities required to develop mature talent. When we understand talent as being about effortful engagement over a long period of time, our focus shifts away from providing opportunity for a few. Instead, we consider the need to engage all children in rigorous activities that require concerted effort in order to maximize capacity in all students, including those we may have overlooked or misunderstood.

It is critical that we consider our fixed mindset way of thinking about intelligence and the way in which it justifies the search for finding potential in very young students. It is critical because, with little information about these young children, the story of the gap supplies an organizing force. The story of the gap fills in that space between facts and conclusions.

When a search for talent among the very young begins before talent has matured, it is based on very little knowledge of students and their capacities. They are five, six, and seven years old and filled with the potential to flourish in ways we cannot now imagine. They are still learning the nuance of laughter and language and growing a foot per year.[24] There is so much missing information, so many unknowns and so much room for confabulation.

One way to counter that tendency-to-fill-in-holes-of-information toward some certainty is to acknowledge how little information one actually has on a young student and instead find certainty in that. Educators can choose to agree that talent is developed over time and not reliably manifest as innate in young students. They can also decide to be certain not about talent identification but of the immense difficulty and error involved with identifying talent at a young age. Moreover, as educators we all can be certain that we don't know for sure. This is to say that we can all decide that *academic data on young students is to be used for formative and instructional planning purposes only*, not to sort students into perceived ability levels.[25]

Another way to counter the reduced level of information about young students is to engage in some level of academic inference and organize those inferences around agreed upon *academic* indicators. We discuss this further in our third recommendation (checklists, see below). For now, recall the many examples where using academic data indicators increased access to formerly disadvantaged students. When educators don't have much information on young students, at least limit and structure the inferences made about these youngsters around academic tasks that are universally available. Doing so will reduce the impact of the gap-story as an organizing force driving interpretations of student academic performance.

As it stands, there is clear and sustained patterns in evidence that missing details about the potentiality of the young are not held at bay or organized around academic performance but are instead filled in by the story of the gap. Systematically, students who are wealthier, White, or Asian American gain advantage and opportunity at the expense of students who are poorer, Black, or Hispanic.[26] Given this reality, it is also critical that educators consider the absurdity of this search for finding potential in young students as a means of nurturing talent.

We challenge educators and community members to reconsider the merit of identifying talent at a young age. Further, we encourage engaging with the idea of purely unstratified, heterogeneous grouping throughout elementary school and preferably through the eighth or ninth grade.

Our premise is simple. We believe that, when the mind is freed of gap-thinking and fixed-intelligence understandings of childhood development, educators can envision a more appropriate and equitable learning context. Identifying problematic mindsets about the intelligence of children allows educators to consider a world where students play and learn together in a mixed array of potentials, passions, and performance. We can imagine a classroom where all students have the opportunity to engage with the full diversity of ideas, experiences, and insights present in their learning community to the advantage of all.

We also recommend that educators free the data and free the mind through better understanding of what the mean in a set of data does not, and cannot, communicate. The mean does not describe the variety and diversity of experience, talent, and present performance levels of individual students.

A shift to understanding the mean for what it is cannot be overemphasized. The simple fact is the mean is one, not great or all-encompassing, way to describe an entire subset of students. A mean does not exactly communicate what is typical. A mean might be derived from a population that sits on the extremes and therefore can even describe an atypical experience. And yet a mean hearkens an imaginary and theoretical student that is then used as a way to understand an entire diverse body of students.

It is with this particular understanding—that a lower mean for a given demographic group does not preclude the existence of a large set of high performers within that group—that we make our final recommendation.

#3 Less Is More: Create Checklists and Then Follow Them

It cannot be overstated that, *if differential experiences are provided for some students and not others*, then individual student objective achievement criteria, and not presumptions based on the mean performance of an entire subgroup, must form the basis for decisions about these course placements for all students.

When it comes to placing students into different mathematics courses, it seems reasonable to assert that students should be evaluated to determine the types of experiences they need to be successful. Often, student strengths and needs can be addressed without resorting to a variety of different high and low mathematical course offerings. Using appropriate tasks and responsive teaching approaches, most students can master the same mathematical content as their peers. This is so even when their peers have different strengths and needs and are thought to be stronger students. This is, indeed, how many countries with high-performance math results do business.[27]

Nevertheless, most school districts in the United States differentiate academic opportunity for students through different course offerings or academic experiences. These differentiated experiences happen throughout elementary school in classrooms and via special services such as academically gifted programs. By middle school, these different academic experiences are generally solidified into different course offerings. One might guess that, if these academic levels are put into place, then students' course-taking opportunities would be based on objective achievement criteria tied to individual student performance. Indeed, the stated objectives for creating different course or class levels are predicated on the academic strengths and needs of individual students.

Unfortunately, while the use of individual academic criteria is a simple and effective approach for identifying students performing at a high level at a given point in time, the academic data becomes confounded by habit, practice, culture, and misplaced judgment. Consistently, students go unrecognized for their exhibited talents and accomplishments because of belief stories, held by adults, that run counter to the data about individual students. Principled guidelines are not sufficient to circumvent the improper use of belief stories held by teachers, counselors, and administrators. What is called for is a more direct approach to determining whether a student meets the criteria for placement into a high-level course. What is needed is the configuration of principled guidelines into a checklist. [28]

Each attribute of success expressed in a set of principled guidelines should be translated into an objective statement about student academic performance that can be judged as having been met or not met. As a result, if the requisite number of objective statements have been met, students would be placed in the high-level class without the interferences of qualifying observations pursuant to beliefs about students' capacity to handle rigorous coursework. In other words, checklist performance data should be honored with appropriate placements *regardless of other characteristics* present in the student.

Because checklists help focus attention on academic performance elements determined to be prerequisite for student success, each behavior may be evaluated cleanly and with less dependence on subjective or holistic interpretations of student performance. Holistic interpretations require inference. For this reason, more holistic approaches (such as teacher or parent referral) are much more prone to the influence of prior beliefs.

Moreover, the use of checklists provides the user with greater confidence that the decisions made as a result of using them is more likely to be accurate, assuming the checklist has been vetted as appropriate and faithful to the established principled guidelines. Adults and students alike can use checklists to evaluate progress and devise strategies to support the academic growth of students. Checklists help everyone better understand the academic goals of programs and provide a foundation for better communicating the teaching and learning objectives of courses and programs.

As a community, all involved (i.e., parents, teachers, building principals, and central office personnel) should work to eliminate criteria that are not specifically related to the academics. Additionally, all should work to remove criteria that relate to "desirable" characteristics of the students, such as their level of effort, organizational habits, ability to focus, or support networks. In other words, do not superimpose ideas about a student's emotional or behavioral constitution, a student's perceived character and potential to achieve, a student's innate intelligence, or a student's family circumstance onto an academic decision. Instead, use *academic* indicators that suggest a student's current level of *academic performance*. After all, it is that performance level, regardless of what advantages students have or what obstacles they have overcome, that should determine opportunity in programs designed to match students' academic performance needs.

We recommend deferring separation of students into different academic tiers. But, if and when a school community adheres to academic separations and differential opportunities, we further recommend a checklist be developed by the educators in that community to determine criteria for placement.[29] Sticking to the maxim that less is more, we recommend that this checklist focus on academic indicators for academic placement.

THE DISCOMFORT, AND REWARD, OF CHANGE

The recommendations for practice we have detailed likely will provoke discomfort in some. And it seems certain that discomfort will spring from the fact that our recommendations require change in the way many teachers and other education professionals work and interact with each other, as well as how they make decisions about students. Based on our experience as teacher educators, we know that change in schools is not easy. Indeed, for various reasons, it is often actively resisted.

For example, some resist change because it challenges and perhaps even contradicts their deeply held beliefs; whereas others resist because the change requires them to abandon attitudes, develop new behaviors, and reconsider and adjust decision-making patterns to which they have become accustomed. Further still, resistance may set in (and various levels of discomfort may be provoked) when the change demands that professionals consider seriously the possibility that they, or their colleagues, have made mistaken judgments about the academic capabilities of a demographic group, or an individual student.

Unfortunately, the data tells us that the latter phenomenon is quite widespread in schools. (Recall from chapter 5 the response of the educators to Alexander's success.) Therefore, we implore educators to dare to make a change in the form of a commitment to equity. Such a commitment means taking demonstrative action to end the scourge on decision-making in contemporary schooling that has resulted in diminished academic opportunities for untold numbers of children and youth.

A central element of the change we champion is for educators to become profoundly discomforted by inequities in the practices and protocols used to place students for instruction. Tracking and other grouping patterns that reflect racial (or socioeconomic status) imbalances and disparities (i.e., classes populated primarily by students from one race/ethnic background) are prime examples. Educators who witness or suspect such imbalances should be prompted to embark on an assessment of the fairness of both formal policies and informal practices that are used in the placement of students for instruction. Often policies allude to (or mention directly) the school's responsibilities for and dedication to high-quality learning experiences for all students. By making a commitment to equity educators hold themselves (and their professional colleagues) to high ethical standards. Doing so means making decisions about student placement for instruction in a way that is in alignment with both the letter and spirit of school or district policy. In a phrase, it means *doing right by* all students.

It is likely that, for at least some educators, to make such a commitment will engender personal doubt brought on by a discomfort with the demands of change, and possibly, a fear of having been wrong about previous decisions. We invite such educators to contemplate the personal growth potential in having been wrong.

> This is the thing about fully experiencing wrongness. It strips us of all our theories, including our theories about ourselves. This isn't fun while it's happening—it leaves us feeling flayed, laid bare to the bone and to the world—but it does make possible that rarest of occurrences: real change. (Schulz, 2010, p. 92)

Ultimately, when educators engage in sincere efforts to understand and improve decision-making in schools—that is, accept the commitment to equity—they can create the space for a new story that permits truly fair opportunity for all. It is our hope that, eventually, we can be certain together that this is the right way to move forward for our children, our society, and our schools.

NOTES

1. Sharot, T. (2017). *The influential mind: What the brain reveals about our power to change others*. New York, NY: Henry Holt and Company, p. 14.
2. Sharot, 2017.
3. This is also known as the affect heuristic. See an explanation of this in Daniel Kahneman, (2013). *Thinking, Fast and Slow*. New York, NY: Farrar, Straus and Giroux, Chapter 13.
4. Sharot, 2017, p. 17.
5. Sharot, 2017, p. 22.
6. See Sharot, 2017, Chapter 1: (Priors) Does Evidence Change Beliefs? The Power of Confirmation and the Weakness of Data. Here, she also explains that our beliefs, and the stories we tell, seem to serve to *deaden* the natural response to error that sparks us to make corrections. Our beliefs can actually reduce our ability to learn from mistakes.
7. Schulz, K. (2010). *Being wrong: Adventures in the margin of error*. New York, NY: HarperCollins.
8. Schulz, 2010, p. 168.
9. Schulz, 2010, p. 164.
10. Schulz, 2010, p. 169.
11. These ideas are drawn from Schulz as discussed throughout her book. In particular, Schulz provides many moving examples of beauty when it comes to the capabilities of the brain, memory, and telling stories. She also discusses and explains inference as it relates to inductive reasoning and the storyteller drive in human beings.

12. In *Being Wrong*, Schulz cites William Hirstein and his 2005 book on confabulation, *Brain Fiction*. Here we use the term as a general phenomenon common to all of us as part of the process of inference and speculation.

13. Kahneman, D. (2011). *Thinking, fast and slow*. New York, NY: Farrar, Straus and Giroux.

14. Sensoy, Ö, & DiAngelo, R. (2017). *Is everyone really equal?* (2nd ed.). New York, NY: Teachers College Press, p. 36.

15. Frederickson also identified Nazi-era Germany and apartheid South Africa as societies with a history of similar orientations to race difference. He described how beliefs about the immutability of race have been utilized historically to explain the permissibility of dissimilar and inferior treatment of particular race groups in otherwise free and democratic societies. The notion of "permanent and unbridgeable" difference made (makes) it possible, acceptable, and lawful for designated "inferior" race groups to be subjected to all manner of exploitation and oppression (including low-quality *inferior schooling*) as contrasted to the treatment, experiences, and life chances accorded individuals belonging to dissimilarly designated (or "superior") race groups.

16. Moule, J. (2009). Understanding unconscious bias and unintentional racism. *Phi Delta Kappan*, *90*(5), 320–326.

17. West, C. (1994). *Race matters*. New York, NY: Vintage Books.

18. See for instance, Rothstein, R. (2017). *The color of law: A forgotten history of how our government segregated America*. New York, NY: Liveright Publishing.

19. Marshall, P. L., Manfra, M. M., & Simmons, C. G. (2016). No more playing in the dark: Twenty-first century citizenship, critical race theory, and the future of the social studies methods course. In A. R. Crowe & A. Cuenca (Eds.), *Rethinking social studies teacher education in the twenty-first century*. New York, NY: Springer International Publishing, p. 68.

20. See Ladson-Billings, G. (1998). Just what is critical race theory and what's it doing in a nice field like education? *Qualitative Studies in Education*, *11*(1), p. 9. Also, King, J. E. (1995). Culture-centered knowledge: Black studies, curriculum transformation, and social action. In J. A. Banks & C. A. McGee Banks (Eds.), *Handbook of research on multicultural education* (pp. 265–290). New York, NY: Macmillan; and Morrison, T. (1992). *Playing in the dark: Whiteness and the literary imagination*. Cambridge, MA: Harvard University Press.

21. See, for example, Delpit, L. (2012). *Multiplication is for White people*. New York, NY: The New Press; Irvine, J. J. (1991). *Black students and school failure*. New York, NY: Praeger; Ladson-Billings, G. (2011). Boyz to men? Teaching to restore Black boys' childhood. *Race Ethnicity and Education*, *14*(1), 7–15; and Perry, T., Steele, C. & Hilliard, A. G. (2003). *Young, gifted, and Black: Promoting high achievement among African-American students*. Boston, MA: Beacon Press.

22. King, J. (1991). Dysconscious racism: Ideology, identity, and the miseducation of teachers. *Journal of Negro Education*, *60*(2), 133–146.

23. These descriptions are based on discussions with hundreds of educators. Early iterations of the arguments in this book are part of a professional development program we have presented for several years in schools across North Carolina as well as formal conference presentations in other states. Along with very personal discussions held through professional development sessions in schools, these conversations also include discussions at conference presentations, including Equity, Math, and the Opportunity Gap: What Does It Mean to Your School? National Conference NCTM in Washington, DC, 2018; Think Less and Do Right: On the Issues of the Achievement Gap, TuffTalk, NC State, February 2016; Opportunity, Equity & Agency: How Do Our Grouping Practices Mediate Student Sense of Mathematical Identity? North Carolina Conference of Teachers of Mathematics, keynote address, 2017; and Equity, Math, and the Opportunity Gap: What Does It Mean to Schools and Systems?, keynote address, Michigan Council of Teachers of Mathematics, 2015.

24. This is poetic license, or you might say, hyperbole. In reality, children grow on average about two to three inches per year.

25. Even further, we agree with the efforts of the San Francisco Unified School District, which now delays tracking in mathematics until students are 15 or 16 years old. For more on this, see the following: Sawchuk, S. (2018, June 12). A bold effort to end algebra tracking

shows promise. Retrieved from https://www.edweek.org/ew/articles/2018/06/13/a-bold-effort-to-de-track-algebra-shows.html. Research data from the district has begun to demonstrate that this approach is not only equitable; it provides the district with a focused approach to curricular and instructional improvement.

26. Consider again the discussion of the at-risk movement found in chapter 2 wherein race and socioeconomic status served to identify students in need of academic help. The logic of the gap (students of color and poorer students perform less well in academics) is used to justify using nonacademic data to identify students in need of academic remediation.

27. Only very isolated school districts in the United States offer rigorous mathematics to all as a policy through middle school. Most recently San Francisco Unified School District has eliminated tracking in eighth grade and mandates that *all* students take algebra in ninth grade and not in middle school. Results of student performance have been positive across demographics, including race and socioeconomic status. See Sawchuk, S. (2018, June 12). A bold effort to end algebra tracking shows promise. Retrieved from https://www.edweek.org/ew/articles/2018/06/13/a-bold-effort-to-de-track-algebra-shows.html.

28. *The Checklist Manifesto*, by Atul Gawande, popularized the idea of a checklist to support medical professionals to act in accordance with medically sound principles. See also: Faulkner, V., Marshall, P. L., Stiff, L. V., & Crossland, C. L. (2017). Less is more: The limitations of judgment. *Phi Delta Kappan*, 98(7), 55–60.

29. Recall from chapter 4 that, if student data presents in a rigid, mean-hugging manner, then the data should not be used as a reliable indicator of student performance and should instead be used to implement institutional change to disrupt created inequities in performance. Therefore, we suggest *the first item on any checklist* be to review data to ensure that there is indeed enough variance in the data to suggest that students have had reasonably sound opportunity to excel.

Appendix

Chapter-by-Chapter Questions

CHAPTER 1

1. In the hockey league example, we saw how coaches of young players appear to identify children for elite play based on relative age. The relative maturity of the players gains them an advantage that is couched in the idea of elite performance. Perhaps identifying the best performers at a given moment in time makes sense if the goal is to win games played by eight-year-olds. But what if the goal is to generate as much talent as possible as children mature into adulthood—how does that change things?

2. The U.S. Club Soccer CEO, Kevin Payne, has said that he believes the system of identifying young players to be put on elite teams is ill-advised. Indeed he states that "I think the whole idea of having aggressive D.A. (Development Academy) expansion below the age of 12—I just think it's dumb. There's no evidence anywhere in any sport in any country to suggest that you can predict the future ability of players before the age of 12 anyway. So, I'm not sure what the point of it is. . . . There is a very small number (of young players) that are being anointed and a very large number that's being told you're not good enough. That's a huge mistake. . . . "[1] And yet these systems persist. What is the story that informs the system of putting young players on "elite" teams to compete with other "elite" players?

3. Consider the Hockey players born in the first quarter of the year.

    a. Why do you think these hockey players (born in the first quarter of the year) seem to be performing less well, once in the NHL, than those born in the last quarter of the year?

b. In your practice or experience, do you see a phenomenon similar to this with regard to student performance in our schools? Or do you think school structure is different? Explain.

4. Consider the Three Pillars as you tell your own story about adult(s)' understandings of you as a child: i) talent is (reliably and meaningfully) detected in the young; ii) talent is innate; and iii) restricted talent pool is desirable. How does your story connect to the Three Pillars? Choose either A or B to respond.

   a. Many of us have a story about adults having a high expectation and understanding of our abilities that did not match our own interests or perception of ourselves. Being a "musical prodigy" in the words of adults, but secretly feeling dispassionate toward music; being called a "math person" but not really understanding math; being called "college material" when you just wanted to paint. What's yours?
   b. Many of us have a story about adults underestimating our abilities and our potential to succeed. Being placed in the "Standard" group when your not-quite-as-clever friend was placed in "Advanced"; being told you were too short, too slow, too unmotivated, to succeed in a sport; receiving less eye contact than other siblings or classmates. What's yours?

CHAPTER 2

1. In the emergency department example, what stories might the doctors have been telling themselves that caused them to resist a change toward a research-tested protocol?
2. Why do you think the doctors may have used descriptive background data (such as weight, gender, race, activity level) to predict an immediate danger better understood through the specifics of immediate heart functioning?
3. What background stories may have impacted an unwitting reliance on gender to choose musicians?
4. What background stories may have impacted an unwitting reliance on body build, a preference for high school players, and a conscious reliance on statistics that measured individual performance (rather than team impact) when scouting players for baseball?
5. Consider the "Data Doppels" you have encountered in your life. Create a list of the ones that come to mind.
6. Consider all you have read in this book through chapter 2. Think of a situation or system within your school, work, or community environ-

ment where you see the complexities of talent development and identification playing out in ways similar to the stories told so far in this book. For instance, you might describe the soccer league structure in your local community, the hiring and promotion protocols at your workplace, the structure of dance classes for young children.

    a. First, describe the current story that justifies this system. As you do so, comment on the spoken and unspoken rationale that supports this system.

    b. Next, reconsider this story:

        i. Does early identification come into play? If not, are there some similar concerns with the identification of talent in this system?

        ii. Does the system serve to increase the talent pool and develop talent in as many people as possible?

        iii. What types of talent/skills/mindsets might be overlooked?

        iv. What latent talents might some people have that you can't see in this situation?

        v. What latent weaknesses might some people have that you can't see in this situation?

        vi. Does the reality of the system match the goals of the current story?

        vii. What might be the key elements of a new system with a different story and rationale?

CHAPTER 3

1. Drawing on data from your State Department of Public Instruction (or other state-level school data clearinghouse), find statistics on the demographics of students and education professionals (teachers, principals) in your state or district. Compare and contrast demographics across five ethnoracial axes (e.g., African American; Asian and Pacific Islander American; Hispanic/Latin America; Native American; White American). How do demographics in your state compare to those noted in table 3.1?

2. As the demographic profile of educators and their students becomes more dissimilar, what specific actions can educators undertake to make the adage "life-long learner" an integral part of their own professional development?

3. Scholars agree that high quality schooling for all students begins with educators rejecting "pathology paradigms" (terminology and frameworks) that directly or indirectly place blame on students for low

quality schooling. In some cases, a slight change in phrasing can prompt new ways of thinking. And of course, new ways of thinking are the forerunners for new ways of acting.

- Consider the term "at risk students" versus the term "students placed at risk." What questions about students, instructional practice, and school policy are prompted by use of the second term (student placed at risk) that are largely not prompted by use of the first term (at risk students)? How might educators' decision-making in regard to instructional placement be affected by a change in terminology?

4. This chapter explores how increasing teacher accountability has inadvertently detracted (and in some respects diminished) teacher professionalism. Drawing on policies and procedures in your own school district, What are some things classroom teachers are being held accountable for that in your judgment extend beyond their role as professional educators? What can teachers do to empower themselves and (re)claim their professionalism?

5. Consider the argument made in chapter 1 that young hockey players would likely benefit from playing with peers who are at different developmental stages than themselves at a given point in time. How might this also apply with students from diverse backgrounds? You may also explore research on bilingual education and empathy development to examine the possibility that greater diversity may actually improve long-term development of students.

CHAPTER 4

1. Consider the "Rigor for All" versus the "Different Strokes" philosophies of education. Which one do you think you hold both in principle and in action? What about your school? Provide evidence and justification (including performance data and placement information) to support your answers.

2. Consider the construct of "giftedness" in education. Tell a personal story that explores how the notion of giftedness impacted your own life and education.

3. Use the figures in chapter 4 to consider the following:

   a. How does the idea of a "gap" in achievement impact the search for high-performing students?

   b. How does the idea of a "gap" in achievement impact an understanding of the "talent pool" available within a population?

c. How does the idea of a "gap" in achievement impact the discussions and decisions made about students?

4. Compare and contrast the idea of "gap-logic" with the idea that individual students perform with great variance and in ways that defy the assumptions made about them. In particular, consider actions taken within your own classroom, school, or district. How do the actions taken line up with the beliefs and assumptions present in the two constructs as discussed in this section and illustrated in chapter 4.

CHAPTER 5

1. Choose the case study from chapter 5 that most resonated for you. *Describe your thoughts and considerations as you read the study.* These can include stories that contained either a personal resonance or a professional resonance.
2. Consider your own role as an educator or community member. How would you advocate for Alexandar, Laila, or the sixth grade students overlooked in the case of Inconsistent Leadership?
3. Explain the thinking and rationale you believe motivated the adults involved in these case studies. This includes a consideration of the thinking and rationales you understood to be advanced by Martin, Joan, Alexander and Laila's teachers and parents, and the principals involved in the different situations.
4. Given these stories, how do you see the role of community members as advocates for high quality educational opportunities for students, and as advocates for equitable policies that support opportunity for all students?
5. Recall a time when you were in a position to disrupt, or call attention to, inequitable habits of behavior and actions. Reflect on your role in this situation. Write about your response/lack of response and then consider and critique your own behaviors and actions.

CHAPTER 6

1. Consider this quote: "The further away data is from one's established beliefs, the less likely it is to be considered valid" (Sharot, p. 31).

    a. Consider yourself and those around you in your non-professional lives. Can you think of examples that support Sharot's claim? Why do you think that is?

      b. Consider yourself and those around you in your professional lives. Can you think of examples that support Sharot's claim? Why do you think that is?

2. Notice your own brain and its confabulations for a non-work day. Jot down notes. What do you hear yourself say? What assumptions do you make about the simplest of things?

3. It is well understood in education circles that educators are motivated to change when they see that the change has a positive impact on their students. But in our experience, represented most specifically by the stories we have told here in chapter 5, this has not held true when it comes to student opportunity in rigorous mathematics course placements. Even when schools and educators have data on the positive impact that providing opportunity for all students has on academic outcomes—policy and practice often does not change.

Given what you have read in chapter 6, consider again the case studies from chapter 5. As you do so, include the ideas of confirmation bias, confabulation, anchoring, and other constructs discussed within chapter 6 to shed light on the stories and motivations of the people within the stories.

      a. Use a case study from chapter 5 to answer the following: What stories are being told that serve as resistance to change? Include specifics about student capabilities and the perceived nature of student actions, habits, and level of performance. You might possibly include explicitly stated ideas about the nature and purpose of advanced mathematics content courses and the nature and purpose of creating different stratifications for student learning.

      b. Use a case study from chapter 5 to answer the following: What stories are not being told that serve as resistance to change? Include unspoken stories about student capabilities and the perceived nature of student actions, habits, and level of performance. You might possibly include unspoken ideas about the nature and purpose of advanced mathematics content courses and the nature and purpose of creating different stratifications for student learning.

      c. Use a case study from chapter 5 to answer the following: What stories did these educators tell themselves about their own intentions, beliefs, and actions? What anchors and available stories may be impacting their decisions? How did these stories impact their relationships, perceptions, and decisions as related to their schools and students? In reflection, have you ever been in a similar situation? Going forward, how might you recognize if you are reacting according to a "story" you rely upon rather than providing students equitable opportunity?

4. Consider your local district, school, or classroom. What data do you have access to that might help you understand trends in your own environment? Consider "math groups," "reading groups," accelerated opportunities, remedial services.

   a. Are there non-academic trends in the students being served?
   b. Find out if clear, objective, criteria were used for placement.

   i. Review the groups being formed using the clear objective data that is stated as the criteria.
   ii. What do you find?
   iii. What stories are told to justify any racial or socioeconomic trends that may be present?
   iv. If there are stories you cited in question iii above, how might these stories be rewritten and how might this impact decision-making and student opportunity?

NOTE

1. https://www.socceramerica.com/publications/article/78918/us-club-soccers-kevin-payne-theres-way-too-m.html

Bibliography

INTRODUCTION

Lubienski, C. A., & Lubienski, S. T. (2013). *The public school advantage: Why public schools outperform private schools.* Chicago, IL: University of Chicago Press.

Rothstein, R. (2017). *The color of law: A forgotten history of how our government segregated America.* New York, NY: Liveright.

CHAPTER 1

Baker, J., & Logan, A. J. (2007). Developmental contexts and sporting success: Birthdate and birthplace effects in National Hockey League draftees 2000–2005. *British Journal of Sports Medicine, 41*(8), 515–517. doi:10.1136/bjsm.2006.033977

Barnsley, R. H., & Thompson, A. H. (1988). Birthdate and success in minor hockey: The key to the NHL. *Canadian Journal of Behavioural Science, 20*(2), 167–176. doi:10.1037/h0079927

Barnsley, R. H., Thompson, A. H., & Barnsley, P. E. (1985). Hockey success and birthdate: The relative age effect. *Canadian Association for Health, Physical Education and Recreation, 51*(8), 23–28.

Brophy, J. E., & Good, T. L. (1970). Teachers' communication of differential expectations for children's classroom performance: Some behavioral data. *Journal of Educational Psychology, 61*(5), 365–374.

Covington, M. V., & Omelich, C. L. (1979). It's best to be able and virtuous too: Student and teacher evaluative responses to successful effort. *Journal of Educational Psychology, 71*(5), 688–700. doi:10.1037/0022-0663.71.5.688

Covington, M. V., & Omelich, C. L. (1985). Ability and effort valuation among failure-avoiding and failure-accepting students. *Journal of Educational Psychology, 77*(4), 446–459. doi:10.1037/0022-0663.77.4.446

Deaner, R. O., Lowen, A., & Cobley, S. (2013). Born at the wrong time: Selection bias in the NHL draft. *PLoS One, 8*(2). doi:10.1371/journal.pone.0057753

Durant, W. (1926). *The story of philosophy.* New York, NY: Garden City.

Dweck, C. S. (2006). *Mindset: The new psychology of success.* New York, NY: Ballantine Books.

Ericsson, K. A., Krampe, R. T., & Tesch-Römer, C. (1993). The role of deliberate practice in the acquisition of expert performance. *Psychological Review, 100*(3), 363–406.

Gardner, H. (1983). *Frames of mind: The theory of multiple intelligences.* New York, NY: Basic Books.

Gladwell, M. (2008). *Outliers: The story of success.* New York, NY: Little, Brown and Company.

Good, T. L. (1987). Two decades of research on teacher expectations: Findings and future directions. *Journal of Teacher Education, 38*(4), 32–47.

Holloway, S. D. (1988). Concepts of ability and effort in Japan and the United States. *Review of Educational Research, 58,* 327–345.

Keefer, Q. A. W. (2015). The sunk-cost fallacy in the National Football League. *Journal of Sports Economics, 18*(3), 282–297. doi:10.1177/1527002515574515

McKown, C., & Weinstein, R. S. (2008). Teacher expectations, classroom context, and the achievement gap. *Journal of School Psychology, 46*(3), 235–261.

Moneymaker effect. (2018, January 22). Retrieved February 10, 2018, from https://en.wikipedia.org/wiki/Moneymaker_effect

Nolan, J. E., & Howell, G. (2010). Hockey success and birthdate: The relative age effect revisited. *International Review for the Sociology of Sport, 45*(4), 507–512. doi:10.1177/1012690210371560.

Stevenson, H. W., & Stigler, J. W. (1992). *The learning gap: Why our schools are failing and what we can learn from Japanese and Chinese education.* New York, NY: Summit Books.

CHAPTER 2

Akos, P., Shoffner, M., & Ellis, M. (2007). Mathematics placement and the transition to middle school. *Professional School Counseling, 10*(3), 238–244.

Banaji, M. R., & Greenwald, A. G. (2013). *Blindspot: Hidden biases of good people.* New York, NY: Delacorte Press.

Berry, R. Q. III, Thunder, K., & McClain, O. L. (2011). Counter narratives: Examining the mathematics and racial identities of Black boys who are successful with school mathematics. *Journal of African American Males in Education, 2*(1), 10–23.

Brown, K. D., Skiba, R. J., & Eckes, S. E. (2009). African American disproportionality in school discipline: The divide between best evidence and legal remedy. *Articles by Maurer Faculty.* Paper 28. Retrieved from http://www.repository.law.indiana.edu/facpub/28

Burris, C. C., Heubert, J. P., & Levin, H. M. (2006). Accelerating mathematics achievement using heterogeneous grouping. *American Educational Research Journal, 43*(1), 105–136.

Doeser, J. (2016, September). *Racial/ethnic and gender diversity in the orchestra field.* Retrieved from http://www.ppv.issuelab.org/resources/25840/25840.pdf

The Education Trust. (2005). *Gaining traction, gaining ground: How some high schools accelerate learning for struggling students.* Washington, DC: Author. Retrieved from https://edtrust.org/wp-content/uploads/2013/10/GainingTractionGainingGround.pdf

The Education Trust–West. (2004). *The A–G curriculum: College-prep? Work-prep? Life prep. Understanding and implementing a rigorous core curriculum for all.* Oakland, CA: Author. Retrieved from https://west.edtrust.org/wp-content/uploads/sites/3/2015/02/College-Prep-Work-Prep-Life-Prep.pdf

Fasang, A. (2006). Recruitment in symphony orchestras: Testing a gender-neutral recruitment process. *Work, Employment and Society, 20*(4), 801–809. doi:10.1177/0950017006069818

Faulkner, V. N., Crossland, C. L., & Stiff, L. V. (2013). Predicting eighth grade algebra placement for students with IEPs. *Exceptional Children, 79*(3), 329–345.

Faulkner, V. N., Stiff, L. V., Marshall, P. L., Nietfeld, J., & Crossland, C. L. (2014). Race and teacher evaluations as predictors of algebra placement. *Journal for Research in Mathematics Education, 45*(3), 288–311.

Garrity, D. (2004). Detracking with vigilance: By opening the high-level doors to all, Rockville Centre closes the gap in achievement and diplomas. *School Administration, 61*(7), 24–27.

Gladwell, M. (2005). *Blink: The power of thinking without thinking.* New York, NY: Little, Brown and Company.

Goldin, C., & Rouse, C. (2000). Orchestrating impartiality: The impact of "blind" auditions on female musicians. *American Economic Review, 90*(4), 715–741. doi:10.1257/aer.90.4.715

Gutierrez, R. (2000). Advancing African American urban youth in mathematics: Unpacking the success of one math department. *American Journal of Education, 109*(1), 63–111.

Hallinan, M. T. (2003). *Ability grouping and student learning.* Brookings Papers on Education Policy. Washington, DC: Brookings Institution Press.

Hoffer, T. B., Rasinski, K. A., & Moore, W. (1995). *Social background differences in high school mathematics and science coursetaking and achievement* (NCES 95-206). National Center for Education Statistics. Washington, DC: U.S. Department of Education.

Johnson, J. L., Campbell, B., Lewis, R., Johnson, J., Redington, M., & Gaal, A. (2005). *North Carolina's school counseling program review: A statewide survey and comprehensive assessment* (Vol. 2006). Raleigh, NC: EDSTAR, Inc.

Kamenetz, A. (2015, April 28). Delinquent. Dropout. At-risk. When words become labels. Retrieved from https://www.npr.org/sections/ed/2015/04/28/399949478/delinquent-dropout-at-risk-whats-in-a-name

Krauss, M. (2016, July 28). Why more women are winning at symphonies' musical chairs. *Denver Post.* Retrieved from https://www.denverpost.com/2016/07/28/why-more-women-are-winning-at-symphonies-musical-chairs/

Lewis, M. (2004). *Moneyball: The art of winning an unfair game.* New York, NY: W. W. Norton & Company.

Martin, D. (2000). *Mathematics success and failure among African-American youth: The roles of sociohistorical context, community forces, school influence, and individual agency.* New York, NY: Routledge.

McGee, E. (2013, February/March). Young, black, mathematically gifted, and stereotyped. *The High School Journal, 96*(3), 253–263.

National Center for Education Statistics, U.S. Department of Education. (2002). *User's manual for the ECLS-K longitudinal kindergarten-first grade public-use data files and electronic codebook.* Retrieved from http://nces.ed.gov/pubsearch/pubsinfo.asp?pubid=2002149

Raible, J., & Irizarry, J. G. (2010). Redirecting the teachers gaze: Teacher education, youth surveillance and the school-to-prison pipeline. *Teaching and Teacher Education, 26*(5), 1196–1203. doi:10.1016/j.tate.2010.02.006

Reilly, B. M., Evans, A. T., Schaider, J. J., Das, K., Calvin, J. E., Moran, L. A., Roberts, R. R., & Martinez, E. (2002). Impact of a clinical decision rule on hospital triage of patients with suspected acute cardiac ischemia in the emergency department. *JAMA, 288*(3), 342–350. doi:10.1001/jama.288.3.342

Seltzer, G. (1989). *Music matters: The performer and the American Federation of Musicians.* Metuchen, NJ: Scarecrow Press.

Skiba, R. J., Horner, R. H., Chung, C., Rausch, M. K., May, S. L., & Tobin, T. (2011). Race is not neutral: A national investigation of African American and Latino disproportionality in school discipline. *School Psychology Review, 40*(1), 85–107. Retrieved from https://proxying.lib.ncsu.edu/index.php/login?url=https://search-proquest-com.prox.lib.ncsu.edu/docview/860230091?accountid=12725

Stiff, L. V., & Johnson, J. L. (2011). Mathematical reasoning and sense making begins with the opportunity to learn. In M. E. Strutchens & J. R. Quander (Eds.), *Focus in high school mathematics: Fostering reasoning and sense making for all students* (pp. 85–100). Reston, VA: National Council of Teachers of Mathematics.

Stiff, L. V., Johnson, J. L., & Akos, P. (2011). Examining what we know for sure: Tracking in middle grades mathematics (pp. 63–76). In W. F. Tate, K. King, & C. Rousseau Anderson (Eds.), *Disrupting tradition: Research and practice pathways in mathematics education.* Reston, VA: National Council of Teachers of Mathematics. Retrieved from https://www.readpbn.com/pdf/Disrupting-Tradition-Research-and-Practice-Pathways-in-Mathematics-Education-Sample-Pages.pdf

Wakin, D. J. (2018, April 11). In American orchestras, more women are taking the bow. *New York Times.* Retrieved from https://www.nytimes.com/2005/07/27/arts/in-american-orchestras-more-women-are-taking-the-bow.html

Wise, B., & Lewin, N. (Writers). (2015). *American orchestras grapple with lack of diversity* [Audio podcast]. Retrieved from https://www.wqxr.org/story/american-orchestras-grapple -diversity/

CHAPTER 3

Alexander, M. (2012). *The new Jim Crow: Mass incarceration in the age of colorblindness.* New York, NY: The New Press.

Apple, M. W., & Jungck, S. (1990). You don't have to be a teacher to teach this unit: Teaching, technology, and gender in the classroom. *American Educational Research Journal, 27*(2), 227–251.

Blackwell, L. S., Trzesniewski, K. H., & Dweck, C. S. (2007). Implicit theories of intelligence predict achievement across an adolescent transition: A longitudinal study and an intervention. *Child Development, 78*(1), 246–263.

Claro, S., Paunesku, D., & Dweck, C. S. (2016). Growth mindset tempers the effects of poverty on academic achievement. *Proceedings of the National Academy of Sciences, 113*(31), 8664–8668.

Cohn, D., & Caumont, A. (2016, March 31). 10 demographic trends that are shaping the U.S. and the world. *Pew Research Center*. Retrieved from http://www.pewresearch.org/fact-tank /2016/03/31/10-demographic-trends-that-are-shaping-the-u-s-and-the-world/

Conant, J. B. (1963). *The education of American teachers.* New York, NY: McGraw-Hill Book Co., Inc.

Delpit, L. (1988). The silenced dialogue: Power and pedagogy in educating other people's children. *Harvard Educational Review, 58*(3), 280–298.

Delpit, L. (2012). *Multiplication is for White people: Raising expectations for other people's children.* New York, NY: The New Press.

Dovidio, J. (2001). On the nature of contemporary prejudice: The third wave. *Journal of Social Issues, 57*(4), 829–849.

Dweck, C. S. (2006). *Mindset: The new psychology of success.* New York, NY: Ballantine Books.

Elkind, D. (2001). *The hurried child: Growing up too fast too soon.* Cambridge, MA: Perseus Publishers.

Faulkner, V. N., Stiff, L. V., Marshall, P. L., Nietfeld, J., & Crossland, C. L. (2014). Race and teacher evaluations as predictors of algebra placement. *Journal for Research in Mathematics Education, 45*(3), 288–311.

Flynn, A., Holmberg, S. R., Warren, D. T., & Wong, F. J. (2017). *The hidden rules of race: Barriers to an inclusive economy.* New York, NY: Cambridge University Press.

Garbarino, J., Bradshaw, C. P., & Vorrasi, J. A. (2002). Mitigating the effects of gun violence on children and youth. *The Future of Children, 12*(2), 72–85.

Griffin, P., & Ouellett, M. (2003). From silence to safety and beyond: Historical trends in addressing lesbian, gay, bisexual, transgender issues in K–12 schools. *Equity & Excellence in Education, 36*(2), 106–114.

Gutstein, E., Lipman, P., Hernadez, P., & de los Reyes, R. (1997). Culturally relevant mathematics teaching in a Mexican American context. *Journal for Research in Mathematics Education, 28*(6), 709–737.

Irvine, J. J. (1991). *Black students and school failure.* New York, NY: Praeger.

Johnson, J., & Stiff, L. (2009). *Who takes honors and advanced placement math?* EDSTAR Analytics, Inc.

King, P. M., & Kitchener, K. S. (2002). The reflective judgment model: Twenty years of research on epistemic cognition (pp. 37–61). In B. K. Hofer and P. R. Pintrich (Eds.), *Personal epistemology: The psychology of beliefs about knowledge and knowing.* Mahwah, NJ: Lawrence Erlbaum & Associates.

Kitchener, K. S., & King, P. M. (1990). The reflective judgment model: Transforming assumptions about knowing (pp. 159–176). In J. Mezirow & Associates (Ed.), *Fostering critical reflection in adults: A guide to transformative and emancipatory learning.* San Francisco, CA: Jossey-Bass.

Koerner, J. D. (1963). *The miseducation of American teachers.* Boston, MA: Houghton Mifflin.

Ladson-Billings, G. (1994). *The dreamkeepers: Successful teachers of African American students.* San Francisco, CA: Jossey-Bass.

Ladson-Billings, G. (1997). It doesn't add up: African American students' mathematics achievement. *Journal for Research in Mathematics Education, 28*(6), 697–708.

Ladson-Billings, G. (2011). Boyz to men? Teaching to restore Black boys' childhood. *Race Ethnicity and Education, 14*(1), 7–15.

Lubienski, C., & Lubienski, S. T. (2014). *The public school advantage: Why public schools outperform private schools.* Chicago, IL: University of Chicago Press.

Marshall, P. L. (2002). *Cultural diversity in our schools.* Belmont, CA: Wadsworth Publishing.

Martin, D. B. (2000). *Mathematics success and failure among African-American youth: The roles of sociohistorical context, community forces, school influence, and individual agency.* Mahwah, NJ: Lawrence Erlbaum Associates.

McIntosh, P. (1988). *White privilege and male privilege: A personal account of coming to see correspondences through work in women's studies.* Wellesley, MA: Wellesley College, Center for Research on Women.

Moule, J. (2009). Understanding unconscious bias and unintentional racism. *Phi Delta Kappan, 90*(5), 320–326.

Mouratidis, A., Michou, A., & Vassiou, A. (2017). Adolescents' autonomous functioning and implicit theories of ability as predictors of their school achievement and week-to-week study regulation and well-being. *Contemporary Educational Psychology, 48*, 56–66.

Murray, O. (2011). Queer youth in heterosexist schools: Isolation, prejudice and no clear supportive policy frameworks. *Multicultural Perspectives, 13*(4), 215–219.

Musu-Gillette, L., de Brey, C., McFarland, J., Hussar, W., Sonnenberg, W., & Wilkinson-Flicker, S. (2017). *Status and trends in the education of racial and ethnic groups 2017* (NCES 2017-051). National Center for Education Statistics. Washington, DC: U.S. Department of Education.

Nasir, N. S., Hand, V., & Taylor, E. V. (2008). Culture and mathematics in school: Boundaries between "cultural" and "domain" knowledge in the mathematics classroom and beyond. *Review of Research in Education, 32*, 187–240.

National Commission on Excellence in Education. (1983). *A nation at risk: The imperative for educational reform.* Washington, DC: U.S. Department of Education.

Oakes, J. (2005). *Keeping track.* New Haven, CT: Yale University Press.

Pew Research Center. (2017). *Hispanic trends.* Retrieved from http://mailchi.mp/pewresearch /w8zd23u60n-2570173?e=b3bf5af499

Reich, K., Culross, P. L., & Behrman R. E. (2002). Children, youth, and gun violence: Analysis and recommendations. *The Future of Children, 12*(2), 4–23.

Rickover, H. G. (1963). *American education, a national failure: The problem of our schools and what we can learn from England.* New York, NY: E.P. Dutton & Co.

Romero, C., Master, A., Paunesku, D., Dweck, C. S., & Gross, J. J. (2014). Academic and emotional functioning in middle school: The role of implicit theories. *Emotion, 14*(2), 227–234.

Sleeter, C. E. (2001). Preparing teachers for culturally diverse schools: Research and the overwhelming presence of whiteness. *Journal of Teacher Education, 52*(2), 94–106.

Tiger, R. (2017). Race, class, and the framing of drug epidemics. *Contexts, 16*(4), 46–51.

Wallitt, R. (2008). Cambodian invisibility: Students lost between the "achievement gap" and the "model minority." *Multicultural Perspectives, 10*(1), 3–9.

Zhao, Y., & Qiu, W. (2009). How good are the Asians? Refuting four myths about Asian-American academic achievement. *Phi Delta Kappan, 90*(5), 338–344.

Zong, J., & Batalova, J. (2017). *Chinese immigrants in the United States.* Retrieved from https://www.migrationpolicy.org/article/chinese-immigrants-united-states

Zumwalt, K., & Craig, E. (2008). Who is teaching? Does it matter? In M. Cochran-Smith, S. Feiman-Nemser, D. J. McIntyre, & K. E. Demers (Eds.), *Handbook of research on teacher education: Enduring questions in changing contexts* (3rd ed., pp. 134–156). New York, NY: Routledge.

CHAPTER 4

Boaler, J. (2015). *Mathematical mindsets: Unleashing students' potential through creative math, inspiring messages and innovative teaching.* San Francisco, CA: Jossey-Bass.

Borland, J. H. (Ed.). (2003). *Rethinking gifted education.* New York, NY: Teachers College Press.

Card, D., & Giuliano, L. (2014). *Does gifted education work? For which students?* (No. w20453). National Bureau of Economic Research.

Card, D., & Giuliano, L. (2015). *Can universal screening increase the representation of low income and minority students in gifted education?* (No. w21519). National Bureau of Economic Research.

Darity, W. A., & Jolla, A. (2009). Desegregated schools with segregated education. In C. Hartman & G. Squires (Eds.), *The integration debate: Competing futures for American cities* (pp. 99–117). New York, NY: Routledge.

Goldsmith, T. (2017, May 24). A Wake schools program helps white, Asian, and male students advance in math. Black, Hispanic, and female students? Not so much. *Indyweek.* Retrieved from https://indyweek.com/news/wake-schools-program-helps-white-asian-male-students-advance-math.-black-hispanic-female-students-much./.

Gould, S. J. (1981). *The mismeasure of man.* New York, NY: W.W. Norton & Company.

Hess, F. M. (2017). *Letters to a young education reformer.* Cambridge, MA: Harvard Education Press.

Hess, R. (2018, June 12). Education reforms should obey Campbell's law. *Education Week.* Retrieved from http://blogs.edweek.org/edweek/rick_hess_straight_up/2018/06/education_reforms_should_obey_campbells_law.html

Long, T., Neff, J., Helms, A. D., & Raynor, D. (2017, May 21). Why have thousands of smart, low-income NC students been excluded from advanced classes? *The News & Observer.* Retrieved from http://www.newsobserver.com/news/local/education/article149942987.html

Sapon-Shevin, M. (1994). *Playing favorites: Gifted education and the disruption of community.* Albany, NY: SUNY Press.

Stevenson, H., & Stigler, J. (1992). *The learning gap: Why our schools are failing and what we can learn from Japanese and Chinese education.* New York, NY: Simon & Schuster.

CHAPTER 5

Akos, P., Shoffner, M., & Ellis, M. (2007). Mathematics placement and the transition to middle school. *Professional School Counseling, 10*(3), 238–244.

Boaler, J. (2006). How a detracked mathematics approach promoted respect, responsibility, and high achievement. *Theory into Practice, 45*(1), 40–46.

Burris, C. C., Heubert, J. P., & Levin, H. M. (2006). Accelerating mathematics achievement using heterogeneous grouping. *American Educational Research Journal, 43*(1), 105–136.

Card, D., & Giuliano, L. (2015). *Can universal screening increase the representation of low income and minority students in gifted education?* (No. w21519). National Bureau of Economic Research.

Dynarski, S. (2016, April 10). Why talented Black and Hispanic students can go undiscovered. *New York Times*, p. BU6.

The Education Trust. (2005). *Gaining traction, gaining ground: How some high schools accelerate learning for struggling students.* Washington, DC: Author. Retrieved from https://edtrust.org/wp-content/uploads/2013/10/GainingTractionGainingGround.pdf

The Education Trust–West. (2004). *The A–G curriculum: College-prep? Work-prep? Life prep: Understanding and implementing a rigorous core curriculum for all.* Oakland, CA:

Author. Retrieved from https://west.edtrust.org/wp-content/uploads/sites/3/2015/02/College-Prep-Work-Prep-Life-Prep.pdf

Garrity, D. (2004). Detracking with vigilance: By opening the high-level doors to all, Rockville Centre closes the gap in achievement and diplomas. *School Administrator, 61*(7), 24–27.

Grissom, J. A., & Redding, C. (2016). Discretion and disproportionality: Explaining the under-representation of high-achieving students of color in gifted programs. *AERA Online, 2*(1), 1–15.

Gutierrez, R. (2000). Advancing African American, urban youth in mathematics: Unpacking the success of one math department. *American Journal of Education, 109*(1), 63–111.

Hallinan, M. T. (2003). Ability grouping and student learning. Brookings Papers on Education Policy. Washington, DC: Brookings Institution Press.

Hoffer, T. B., Rasinski, K. A., & Moore, W. (1995). *Social background differences in high school mathematics and science coursetaking and achievement* (NCES 95-206). National Center for Education Statistics. Washington, DC: U.S. Department of Education.

Mayer, A. (2008). Understanding how U.S. secondary schools sort students for instructional purposes: Are all students being served equally? *American Secondary Education, 36*(2), 7–25.

McGrath, D. J., & Kuriloff, P. J. (1999). "They're going to tear the doors off this place": Upper-middle-class parent school involvement and the educational opportunities of other people's children. *Educational Policy, 13*(5), 603–629.

Oakes, J., & Wells, A. S. (1998). Detracking for high student achievement. *Education Leadership, 55*(6), 38–41.

Sawchuk, S. (2018, June 12). A bold effort to end algebra tracking shows promise. Retrieved from https://www.edweek.org/ew/articles/2018/06/13/a-bold-effort-to-de-track-algebra-shows.html

Stiff, L. V., & Johnson, J. L. (2011). Mathematical reasoning and sense making begins with the opportunity to learn. In M. E. Strutchens & J. R. Quander (Eds.), *Focus in high school mathematics: Fostering reasoning and sense making for all students* (pp. 85–100). Reston, VA: National Council of Teachers of Mathematics.

CHAPTER 6

Delpit, L. (2012). *Multiplication is for White people.* New York, NY: The New Press.

Faulkner, V., Marshall, P. L., Stiff, L. V., & Crossland, C. L. (2017). Less is more: The limitations of judgment. *Phi Delta Kappan, 98*(7), 55–60.

Gawande, A. (2010). *The checklist manifesto.* New Delhi, India: Penguin Books India.

Irvine, J. J. (1991). *Black students and school failure.* New York, NY: Praeger.

Kahneman, Daniel. (2013). *Thinking, fast and slow.* New York, NY: Farrar, Straus and Giroux.

King, J. (1991). Dysconscious racism: Ideology, identity, and the miseducation of teachers. *Journal of Negro Education, 60*(2), 133–146.

King, J. E. (1995). Culture-centered knowledge: Black studies, curriculum transformation, and social action. In J. A. Banks & C. A. McGee Banks (Eds.), *Handbook of research on multicultural education* (pp. 265–290). New York, NY: Macmillan.

Ladson-Billings, G. (1998). Just what is critical race theory and what's it doing in a nice field like education? *Qualitative Studies in Education, 11*(1), 7–24.

Ladson-Billings, G. (2011). Boyz to men? Teaching to restore Black boys' childhood. *Race Ethnicity and Education, 14*(1), 7–15.

Marshall, P. L., Manfra, M. M., & Simmons, C. G. (2016). No more playing in the dark: Twenty-first century citizenship, critical race theory, and the future of the social studies methods course. In A. R. Crowe & A. Cuenca (Eds.), *Rethinking social studies teacher education in the twenty-first century.* New York, NY: Springer International Publishing.

Morrison, T. (1992). *Playing in the dark: Whiteness and the literary imagination.* Cambridge, MA: Harvard University Press.

Moule, J. (2009). Understanding unconscious bias and unintentional racism. *Phi Delta Kappan, 90*(5), 320–326.

Perry, T., Steele, C., & Hilliard, A. G. (2003). *Young, gifted, and Black: Promoting high achievement among African-American students*. Boston, MA: Beacon Press.

Rothstein, R. (2017). *The color of law: A forgotten history of how our government segregated America*. New York, NY: Liveright Publishing.

Sawchuk, S. (2018, June 12). A bold effort to end algebra tracking shows promise. Retrieved from https://www.edweek.org/ew/articles/2018/06/13/a-bold-effort-to-de-track-algebra-shows.html

Schulz, K. (2010). *Being wrong: Adventures in the margin of error*. New York, NY: Harper-Collins.

Sensoy, Ö., & DiAngelo, R. (2017). *Is everyone really equal?* (2nd ed.). New York, NY: Teachers College Press.

Sharot, T. (2017). *The influential mind: What the brain reveals about our power to change others*. New York, NY: Henry Holt and Company.

West, C. (1994). *Race matters*. New York, NY: Vintage Books.

Index

ability, 7, 17n1; academics and, 31; cause
and, 36; effort and, 18n22–18n23;
homogeneous ability grouping, 50–51,
60n19; identification of, 7; perceptions
of, 119
academic achievement, 14
academic achievement gap, 1, 117, 124n23
academic knapsack, 48, 60n13
academics, 14, 31, 119; criteria and, 120;
data and, 30; opportunity and, 65
access, 66, 91, 96; Black students and, 94;
equity and, 101; giftedness and, 69;
inequities and, 72, 92; opportunity and,
71; personnel and, 80; variability and,
102
accountability, 49–50, 50, 53
accuracy, 121
achievement-gap mean, 75–78
admissions, 94
adults, 93
advocacy, 93, 94
African American students. *See* Black
students
airlines, 73
Akos, Patrick, 100
anchoring, 110
Asian American students, 41n49, 70
assessments, 50
assumptions, 11–12
at-risk movement, 30–32, 125n26
attributes, 121

auditions, 25–26, 39n21
autonomy, 53

baseball, 26–28, 39n26, 40n28
behavior, 55, 98
belief, 14, 19n25; change and, 105–123;
cultural norms and, 111–113; data
versus, 87, 99–101, 102; death penalty
and, 107; professionals and, 88–89;
recommendations and, 96, 103n8
belief stories, 105; merit-based, 117
benefits, 10
bias, 2, 94; discipline and, 55; research on,
55
Black students, 34, 76, 115; access and, 94;
decision-making and, 112; opportunity
and, 35; performance and, 35, 56;
placement and, 70
Borland, James, 69, 82n15–82n17

Campbell's Law, 72–74, 83n36
capacities, 67
case studies, 102n1
cause, 32, 36, 38n3
certainty, 108–113
change, 105–123
characteristics, 72; demographics and, 31,
58n3; placement and, 121
checklists, 120–122
children, 29, 118; mindsets of, 52;
opportunity gap and, 48–50

elitism, 15; effort and, 15; policy and, 90
Elkind, David, 48, 59n11
End-of-Course exam (EOC), 96
end-of-grade assessment (EOG), 33
engagement, 123; adjustments and, 89–90;
    children and, 118
EOC. *See* End-of-Course exam
EOG. *See* end-of-grade assessment
equity, 101
Ericsson, K. Anders, 12
ethics, 115
ethnoracial diversity, 46
EVAAS. *See* Education Value-Added
    Assessment System
exceptionality, 7
expectations, 29, 90; performance and, 15,
    19n31
experiences, 120; schools and, 1;
    wrongness and, 123

fact-checking, 109
factories, 73
failure, 3
families, 73
family composition, 47, 59n5
fixed mindset, 51; grouping and, 57;
    intelligence and, 118
flight times, 73
Frederickson, George, 113, 124n15

gap-logic, 75, 125n26; invocation of, 80
gap-making, 7; data and, 21–38; decision-
    making and, 53–54; identification of,
    17; phenomenon of, 45
gaps, 11, 116; academic achievement, 1;
    data and, 117; mathematics and, 1;
    source of, 33; unnatural occurrence of,
    117
Gardner, Howard, 17n1
gifted education, 65; Asian American
    students and, 70; Borland on, 69,
    82n15–82n17
giftedness: access and, 69; history and,
    67–68; identification and, 68, 70; public
    schools and, 82n10; SES and, 72,
    82n23
girls, 101
goals, 67, 90; understanding of, 2
Goldin, C., 25–26

Goldman Index, 23–25
grades, 98
graphs, 11; interpretations and, 117; mean
    and, 120
Greece, 57
grouping, 119
growth mindset, 7; characterization and,
    51; decision-making and, 56–57
gun violence, 47; school shootings and,
    59n7

habits, 18n21; assumptions and, 80; culture
    and, 17; practice and, 71
heart attacks, 23–25
Hess, Richard, 72–73
heuristics, 115
high schools, 97; stratification and, 100
high stakes, 50; accountability and, 53
Hispanic students, 70
history, 81n1; data and, 28; giftedness and,
    67–68
hockey, 10, 41n38; context of, 15
homogeneous ability grouping, 50–51,
    60n19
human brain: duality and, 109; stories and,
    109
hurrying childhood, 48, 59n11

idea, 23; data and, 106; disruption and,
    111, 125n29; intelligence as, 68; talent
    as, 12, 18n17; of variety, 77
identification, 75; ability and, 7; gap-
    making and, 17; giftedness and, 68, 70;
    mindset and, 51–52; of patients, 24;
    systems of early, 9, 16
illogic, 32
imagination, 109
immigrants, 46
impact, 1, 26, 39n20, 118; cumulative
    impact, 99
improvement, 34
inequities, 35, 116; access and, 72, 92;
    gifted education and, 69; placement
    and, 81; resolution of, 71; responsibility
    and, 71
influence, 56
information, 108, 119
intelligence, 68, 118
interpretations, 117, 124n23

About the Authors

Valerie Faulkner is an associate teaching professor at North Carolina State University, where she focuses on K–2 mathematics instruction and issues of equity. She has received the North Carolina State College of Education Outstanding Teacher Award, North Carolina State Alumni Association Outstanding Teaching Award, and the North Carolina State Chancellors Creating Community Outstanding Faculty Award. She has published articles in the *Journal of Research in Mathematics Education, Phi Delta Kappan, Teaching Children Mathematics, Teacher Education and Special Education, Exceptional Children*, and *Australian Primary Mathematics Classroom*. Her 2012 TEDxNCSU lecture, "Teaching Math to the Analog Brain in the Digital World," was chosen as a TEDx lecture of the month by TED. Her background includes 17 years as a teacher in North Carolina public schools.

Patricia L. Marshall is a professor in the Department of Teacher Education and Learning Sciences at North Carolina State University. She is a member of the NC State University Academy of Outstanding Teachers. Her writings have appeared in various venues, including the *Journal of Teacher Education, Journal of Educational Research, The Educational Forum, Journal of Urban Mathematics Education*, and *International Journal of Multicultural Education*. Her books include *Cultural Diversity in Our Schools* and *When Critical Multicultural Education Meets Mathematics: A Mixed Methods Study of Professional Development and Teacher Identity* (with DeCuir-Gunby and McCulloch). She is a Fulbright Scholar, having received a teaching and research core award to Ecuador, and was awarded the Carl A. Grant Research Award from the National Association for Multicultural Education.

Lee V. Stiff is professor of mathematics education at North Carolina State University and has taught mathematics in grades K–12. He received the Rankin Memorial Award for Excellence in Mathematics Education, the Fulbright Scholar Award to the University of Ghana, and the 2019 NCTM Lifetime Achievement Award. From 2000 to 2002, he was president of the National Council of Teachers of Mathematics (NCTM). He is president of Edstar Analytics, a consulting firm providing schools with data-driven decision models for student success and teacher effectiveness. Dr. Stiff has coauthored several math textbooks.